BY VINCE SPEZZANO
...from paperboy to president of USA Today

**Cover and cartoons by
Jim "GOOT" Guttenberg**

This book is dedicated to my wife and friend, Marge for 47 years of reasons.

Book Design & Typography by:
Guttenberg Press Publications
FAX: (407) 639-5695

ISBN: 1-878398-55-5

PUBLISHED BY
Blue Note Books
(407) 799-2583, FAX (407) 799-1942
1-800-624-0401

Printed in the United States of America

The Contents

Marjorie Elliott Spezzano

Foreword

Vince has been sharing his jokes with audiences and friends for many years. With this book he hopes to reach a larger audience and make more friends.

— **Marge Spezzano**

About The Author

MEET VINCE SPEZZANO

Who is Vince Spezzano, and how did he amass such a collection of humor? Vincent Edward Spezzano retired May 1991 as chairman of both the Gannett Rochester Newspapers and *Florida TODAY*, after 36 years with Gannett Company, Inc.

A native of Retsof, New York (a village near Rochester), he served as a U.S. Navy volunteer during World War II before pursuing higher education. He earned his B.A. in Journalism and English at Syracuse University, following two years of study in civil engineering.

His newspaper career ranged from paperboy to top management. Spezzano's second newspaper job was on the weekly newspaper, *Livingston Republican*, in

Geneseo, New York (the first, of course, was as a youthful paperboy). Hired as a police reporter for the *Lynchburg Daily News*, he moved from Lynchburg, Virginia to St. Louis, Missouri and the *Globe-Democrat* as a general reporter. From there, he made the jump to the Gannett Company, hired as a reporter on *The Times-Union* in Rochester.

He moved steadily upward in his career with Gannett...from police reporter to political columnist, from public service director to senior vice president of communications, on to President of *USA TODAY* and *USA Today International*. He also served as a Gannett Company director and headed the task force that developed the concept for *USA TODAY*.

He has twice been nominated for Pulitzer Prizes and has received countless honors and awards, including: the Silver Shovel of the International Newspaper Promotion Assn.; twice honored as Citizen of the Year in Rochester, New York; Communicator of the Year; and, was confirmed to the Order of the Cavaliere (Knight) from Italy.

He has been listed in *Who's Who in America* for nearly two decades and also is listed in *Who's Who in The East, in the South, Finance and Industry, and International Businessmen.*

A myriad of volunteer positions, both professionally and in community service, have honed his speaking skills. Spezzano has been a speaker and master of ceremonies in the USA, Canada, Mexico, Europe, Japan and at a dozen colleges and universities before audiences ranging in size from nine to 7,000.

Over the years as a guest speaker, he has compiled an enormous collection of humor. It is not unusual, even now in his retirement, to get an urgent call from someone needing jokes, anecdotes or truisms to "break the ice", "hook the audience", or make an effective closing for "their" speech.

At 71 years of age, he is the father of two sons and a daughter. He lives in Cocoa Beach, Florida with his wife, Marjorie Elliott Spezzano. Active in community service, he serves on seven community boards. He fills his leisure hours with golf, tennis, an occasional newspaper column and is presently working on a novel about the media world and its people.

Introduction

As a speaker for most of my 35 years in the newspaper business (in positions ranging from reporter to President of *USA Today*), I was always looking for light material to help the heavy stuff go down.

This book has been produced for people who are looking for ideas – light material to help the heavy stuff go down and to get and hold their audience's attention. In it can be found ideas: jokes, ancedotes and truisms that they can use in business, in everyday life and for their enjoyment.

It was produced by hundreds who have contributed humor or wisdom (whether they knew I was listening or not).

Over the years I've been writing down most of the jokes I've heard and I've collected some of the best.

My 70th birthday prompted me to dig into my computer, desk drawers and files, and get them organized into categories. I'm hoping you'll find something for every occasion.

My thanks to My Friend Marge, My Artist Goot, His Friend Charlotte, who made this book possible, all My Friends – and everybody else.

Age

❤An adult is a person who has stopped growing except in the middle.

❤At the age of fifty one settles down into certain well-defined convictions, most of which are wrong.

❤"I was so cold last night I couldn't sleep. I just lay there and shivered."

"Did your teeth chatter?"

"I don't know — we don't sleep together."

❤A woman was filling out an application for credit. When she came to the space for age she hesitated a long time. Finally the clerk leaned over and said: "The longer you wait the worse it gets."

❤The worst thing about getting old is listening to the children's advice.

❤Many a middle-aged woman is thick and tired of it.

❤An old-timer is one who remembers when a baby-sitter was called mother.

❤Hardening of the heart ages people more quickly than hardening of the arteries.

❤When you're over 50, you have good news and bad news. The bad news is, you can no longer understand the lyrics to popular songs. The good news is, you can no longer understand the lyrics to popular songs.

❤I'm at that age where all I want to be is independently

healthy.

♥Sixty is when you come out of the shower, look at yourself in a full-length mirror and realize the awesome power of gravity.

♥You learn two things as you grow older. The first is that money isn't everything. The second is that everything isn't everything.

♥Sixty is when you get socks, underwear and earmuffs for Christmas – and you're glad.

♥I've reached that mid-point in life somewhere between The Blue Lagoon and Golden Pond.

♥Youth is when you wonder if your watch is too fast. Middle-age is when you wonder if your calendar is.

♥I'm at that age where I keep publications like *PLAY-BOY* at arm's length. It's the only way I can get them in focus.

♥It's kinda discouraging. By the time you get used to being middle-aged – you're old.

Business

❤There's a lot of problem hiring people these days. You can't ask in advance about a person's sex. And sometimes, after the interview, you still don't know.

❤The boss always says anything goes. This morning he started calling me anything.

❤Our sales department likes our products so well, they hate to part with them.

It is verified that the Liberty Bell cracked on July 8, 1835. It is probable that the warranty expired the day before.

❤A retirement dinner is the last opportunity an employee has to be fed up by the company.

❤It's amazing how much permanent confusion can be caused by a temporary secretary.

❤Businessmen should be careful on long trips. Jet lag is when your briefcase arrives a day ahead of your brain.

❤Panic is that subtle emotion you feel when you realize your business has three more salesmen than customers.

❤When we hire a salesman, we always use the ink-blot test. We show each applicant an ink-blot and the first one who tries to sell us a new pen, gets the job.

❤For the last six years I've been getting memos from THE DESK OF JOE JONES. Last month Joe Jones retired and I'm really broken up. I never cared for Jones too much – but his desk I really miss.

❤One company has a new policy designed to attract young people. It's called on-the-job retirement.

❤It's very important to work twelve hours a day, seven days a week, and never take any vacations. How else are you going to finance your heart attack?

❤I don't want to complain, but the economy is really ruining my love life. I love money.

❤If you think athletes exaggerate the importance of the home-field advantage, ask yourself this question: How many times have you won in the boss's office?

❤Is it true that in college, as part of higher mathematics, they teach Einstein's Theory of Relativity? And if you master that, they go on to annual reports.

❤I once belonged to a union that had a dental plan. If you paid your dues you got to keep your teeth.

❤It's very disconcerting when the boss calls you his right-hand woman – and you know he's left-handed.

❤Why is it that one of the biggest ambitions of a $100,000 a year executive is to have a $250 a week maitre d' know her name?

❤When she left her last job, they had nothing but good things to say about her: Goodbye and good riddance!

❤I try to help. I read that one small country was looking for mercenaries so I sent them the name of my plumber, my used car salesman, my TV repairman, and my son's orthodontist.

❤They say that many people have just given up looking for work. I know about our sales staff. Who are the rest.

❤Mexico also has enormous reserves of natural gas. It's found in three principal locations – tamales, enchiladas and burritos.

❤A business slowdown is the pause that depresses.

❤Americans are dedicated to the concept of conservation. Americans also shave with two blades at the same time.

❤Let us never forget the immortal words of General Robert E. Lee, when he turned to his troops and said, "Men – look for the Union Label!"

❤This is the time of year when things long dormant come to life. Now if we can only convince our sales department.

♥A man whose work pattern has inspired the Payroll Department to come up with a brand new classification: On-The-Job Retirement.

♥I've come to this conclusion,
It's one I've long supposed;
The boss's door is open -
It's his mind that's always closed.

♥Everything is relative. To a June graduate, B.A. stands for Bachelor of Arts. To a July employer, it stands for Barely Able.

♥It's very discouraging to see what deficit spending has done to interest rates. The more we prime the pump, the more it pumps the prime.

♥Columbus is the one who came ashore and said, "I claim this land for the King and Queen of Spain" - and it really suprised the Indians because they didn't even know they had listed it.

♥When a builder advertises a new house as a "steal", I wish they'd define who is the stealer and who is the stealee.

♥There's nothing wrong with doing business with someone you don't trust as long as you don't trust him.

♥I don't want to complain, but I have suitcases that have travelled 9,000 more miles than I have.

♥I'll say one thing for this job: Not only does it give you a pension, but it also helps you to age a lot faster.

♥I asked one job applicant what he could do and he said, "Nothing." I didn't hire him. If there's one thing I hate it's somebody who's after my job.

❤Personally, I look forward to retirement. I will always think of 65 as not a working number.

❤For a while, it just didn't look as if I was going to fit into the newspaper business. For instance, my whole first year I had to apologize for coming in to work sober.

❤The trouble with being in public relations is, you are always on call. You're looking at the only fella in history who was ever operated on for an ingrown beeper.

❤This morning I had a long talk with the boss. Actually, he had a long talk. I had a long listen.

❤Annual reports are four color, 48 page booklets printed on 28 pound coated stock with die-cut vellum covers – that tell you how management is fighting to keep down costs.

❤You can learn a lot about a company just by looking at its annual report. For instance, the more pictures, the-less profits.

❤An annual report is almost religious in its format. It's where the Report from the Chairman of the Board giveth – and the Notes to Financial Statements taketh away.

❤We also had a little problem with our stockroom clerk. Frankly, we didn't realize we had a problem until our last inventory – which we had to take in his basement.

❤I was saying that this summer I'd like to get away from it all and go someplace where no one would ever think to find me. The boss suggested my desk.

❤They have such high-sounding phrases today, like

"management by objective." Years ago we also had management by objective. The objective was to keep your job.

❤Your Sales Department is the key to whether you win or lose. Beware the group whose pants wear out much earlier than their shoes.

❤Advertising is where the typical thirty year career goes like this: You start off by being the youngest person in the office – and you wind up by working for the youngest person in the office.

❤Personally, I think it's been a very good year – if we exclude everything up to today.

❤Computers are so incredibly intelligent, fast and accurate, sometimes I wonder how we were ever able to build one without one.

❤Have you noticed how everybody seems to have a preconceived notion of how bachelors live? That's right. Last night a strange woman came up to me and whispered that she'd come up to my apartment for fifty dollars – and clean it.

❤I'll tell you how bad things are. Last week I was laid off. And I'm self-employed.

❤I asked our accountant how we were doing and he said, "I can give you the same odds God gave to Noah. You've got forty days and nights to keep from going under."

❤There is only one sure way to achieve job security: Have the boss make a hole-in-one and you're the only witness.

♥Do you ever get the feeling your Sales Department couldn't sell batteries on Christmas morning?

♥You know you're in trouble when the person who comes to foreclose on your house – drives up in your repossessed car.

♥I had good news and bad news out at the airport today. The good news is that the first two pieces of luggage out of the baggage chute were mine. The bad news is, they started off as one piece.

♥Bosses are contagious. You catch hell from them.

♥I retired four years ago. My biggest problem is keeping the boss from finding out.

♥Never be totally candid with your boss until he's retired – or you are.

♥Advertising is the fine art of convincing you that debt is better than frustration.

♥A waiter was horrified to see a patron washing his spoon in the fingerbowl. "Why, are you washing your spoon in the fingerbowl," asked the waiter.
 "Because I don't want to get ice cream all over my pocket," replied the diner.

♥An executive is a man who can take two hours for lunch without hindering production.

♥"Thirty dollars to paint my garage? That's outrageous! I wouldn't pay Michelangelo that much to paint my garage!" "Listen, you," said the painter, "if he does the job for any less, we'll come and picket yer place!"

♥Only a week after he started work, he announced he was quitting.

"It isn't the pay," he explained to the foreman. "It's just that I can't help having a guilty conscience."

"What for?" asked the foreman.

"All the time I'm worrying about how I'm cheating some big, strong mule out of a job."

❤A young man dashed into the electrician's shop, his face flushed with anger. "Didn't I ask you yesterday morning to send a man to mend our doorbell?" he roared. "And did you not promise to send him around at once?"

"But we did, sir," broke in the manager. "I'm quite sure of it! Hi, Bill!" he called to one of his workmen at the back of the office. "Didn't you go round to Park Lodge yesterday to do that job?"

"Yes sir," replied Bill. "I went round all right, and I rang the bell for over ten minutes, but I couldn't get no answer, so I guessed they must not be at home."

❤The best things in life are still free, but the tax experts are working overtime on the problem.

❤A storekeeper had two clerks, Jim and Albert. Albert, whose home was a mile from the store, always arrived on time for the day's work. Jim, who lived in a room above the store, was usually late.

One day the storekeeper remarked to Jim, with some asperity, "It's a funny thing. Albert, who lives a mile away, can always get here on time, while you, who live right here, are nearly always late."

"Nothing funny about that," replied Jim. "If Albert wakes up late, he can always put on a burst of speed.

But if I'm late, I'm already here."

❤A recession is when you see the plumber's truck in your driveway – and hope your wife is having an affair.

❤Old gardeners never die; they just spade away.

❤The manager of a hotel, finding that a guest had departed without paying his hotel bill, wrote him: "My dear Mr. Smith: Will you please send the amount of your bill." To this Mr. Smith wrote: "My dear Mr. Manager: The amount of my bill is a hundred and ten dollars. Yours respectfully."

❤Barber: The village gosnip.

❤More important than the time you get up in the morning is the time you get down to work.

❤An executive is a man who is able to have everything he needs charged.

❤Executive ability — The faculty of earning your bread by the work of other people.

❤Genius is the ability to evade work by doing something right the first time it has been done.

❤The trouble with these "How to Succeed" books is that you find out from them that you have to work for it.

❤He was the kind of office manager who took criticism like a man. He blamed it on his associates.

❤A far sighted office employee is one who asks for a desk away from the door so she won't get killed at five o'clock.

❤The business man who demands facts in his office buys hair restorer from a bald-headed barber.

❤Economics Simplified: When buyers do not fall for prices, prices must fall for buyers.

❤Save your pennies and the sales tax will take care of them.

❤The butcher informed a customer: "I can't give you any more credit. Your bill is bigger than it should be."

"I know that," said the customer. "Just make it out for what it should be, and I'll pay it."

❤The man with the hoe doesn't get nearly as far as the man with the hokum.

❤The son of a Harvard professor, recently inducted into the army, sneaked off to sit behind the barracks and rest. He was discovered by a grizzled old sergeant who demanded: "What are you doin' back here?"

 The guilty recruit stammered, "I'm procrastinating, sir."

 The sergeant thought about this for a time and barked, "Well, O.K., just keep busy!"

❤A go-getter who becomes his own boss is apt to wind up a nervous wreck.

❤A loafer is a person who spends his time keeping busy people idle.

❤The turn-over is highly important whether it is in business or right after the alarm clock goes off in the morning.

❤Bob describes his butcher as a clumsy fellow whose hands are always in the weigh.

❤Baby sitters: girls you hire to watch your television set.

❤The office drinking fountain —"Old Faceful."

❤Boss: "O.K. now, gang, let's take a ten-minute break for work!"

❤Millions of American commuters live in a clock-eyed world.

❤*Manager of the store:* "Been to the zoo, yet, sonny?"
New Delivery Boy: "No, sir."
Manager: "Well, you should. You'll enjoy it, and get a big kick out of watching the turtles zip by."

❤Correspondence in a business effciency magazine has been discussing how to stop a typist talking. Our own method is to ask her to read back from her shorthand.

❤Business is always improving for the beauty parlor operator.

❤Business never comes back unless you go after it.

❤Eight years working for the firm — never absent, never late — then one morning he came in an hour and a half late, his clothes torn, his face and hands scratched and bloody.
Boss: "Why are you late?"
"I leaned out the window and fell three stories!"
Boss: "That took you an hour and a half?"

❤About the only thing the farmers don't raise enough of is farm hands.

❤A white collar man is one who carries his lunch in a briefcase instead of a pail.

❤The person who puts up the billboards on country roads must have some sense of beauty because they always pick out the best views to obstruct.

❤*Efficiency Expert:* "Mr. Jones, what do you do here?"
Jones: "Nothing."
Efficiency Expert: "And, Mr. Martin what do you do here?"
Martin: "Nothing."
Efficiency Expert: "Hmmm. Duplication."

❤The new office boy had neglected his duties and his employer decided to give him a reminder.

"Belsen," he began, "I wrote your name with my finger in the dust on my desk this morning."

"Yeah, boss, I know," the youth replied, "and you spelled it wrong."

❤Trying to rest after a hard day, poor father was being annoyed by an endless stream of questions from Willie.

"What did you do all day at your office, Daddy?"

"Nothing!" shouted the father.

After a thoughtful pause, Willie asked, "Dad, how do you know when you're through?"

❤"Do you mean to say you worked all night? I wouldn't have dreamed of it."

"Neither would I — the boss thought of it."

❤A kangaroo sat down at a drug counter and ordered a lemonade. The clerk served the drink. The kangaroo reached for it, then dropped his paw suddenly.

"Where's the red cherry?" asked the unusual customer. The clerk supplied it promptly.

"Strange, isn't it?" a man whispered to the clerk.

"Yes, it is," said the latter. "It's the first time in five years that I forgot to put a red cherry in a lemonade."

❤Then there was the gunman who walked up to a theatre cashier, stuck a gun in her face, and growled: "The picture was horrible — give me everybody's money back."

❤One of the great educational challenges of our time is convincing an auto mechanic that something that badly needs fixing isn't the same as something that needs fixing badly.

❤Some people are always taking the joy out of life and a good many of them are in the Internal Revenue Department.

❤*Boss:* "I wish you wouldn't whistle at your work."
Clerk: "I wasn't working."

❤*Sylvia:* "When I applied for a job the manager had the nerve to ask if my punctuation was good."
Mildred: "What did you tell him?"
Sylvia: "I said I'd never been late for work in my life."

❤*Attendant:* "I'm sorry, sir, but all business at this service station is strictly cash."
Motorist: "But the sign says plainly, 'Batteries Charged.'"

❤"Why did you fire that secretary you had?"
"She couldn't spell — kept asking me how to spell every other word when she took dictation."
"And you couldn't stand the interruptions?"
"It wasn't that. I just didn't have time to look up all those words."

❤I always do my hardest work before breakfast.
What's that?

Getting up.

❤ *Marge:* "If your folks won't consent to your marrying Jack, why don't you elope?"

Minnie: "No chance. Jack's a painter and he won't climb a ladder after 4:30 P.M."

❤ *First Steno:* "Yes, the boss is mean all right, but he's fair."

Second Steno: "What do you mean he's fair?"

Third Steno: "He's mean to everyone."

❤ Public relations is the fine art of making sure that something is no sooner done than said.

❤ Success is when you're working on your second million and the IRS is working on your first.

❤ The worst job you can have in any organization is Treasurer – because, no matter what is proposed, you have to think of it in terms of money. I'm firmly convinced that if our Treasurer had arranged for the Last Supper – there would have been a cash bar.

❤ If you don't think PR works, consider the millions and millions and millions of Americans who now think yogurt tastes good.

❤ I'm willing to let that Alabama telephone user speak for all of us. The one who said: "The only thing ah have against Ma Bell is mah bill!"

❤ "Operator, I'd like to report an obscene phone bill!"

❤ A farmer in great need of extra hands at harvest time finally asked Si, who was accounted the town fool, if he could help him out.

"What'll ye pay?" asked Si.

"I'll pay you what you're worth," answered the farmer. Si scratched his head a minute, then answered decisively: "Don't believe I'll work for that!"

❤It is always easy to covet another man's success without envying his labors.

A lioness saw her young cub chasing a hunter around a bush. The lioness growled and said, "Junior, how often do I have to tell you not to play with your food."

Cooking

❤A husband, complaining about the food, was met with a strong argument by his wife.

"What's the matter with you?" she demanded. "Monday you liked beans, Tuesday you liked beans, Wednesday you liked beans; now Thursday, all of a sudden, you don't like beans!"

❤Two cannibals met in a hut. One was tearing out pictures of men, women, and children from a magazine—stuffing them into his mouth and eating them.

"Tell me," said the other. "Is that dehydrated stuff any good?"

❤When a diner complained that he couldn't eat the soup that had been brought him, the waiter called the manager.

"I'm very sorry, sir," said the manager, "I'll call the chef."

When the chef arrived, the diner still insisted that he couldn't eat his soup.

"What's wrong with it?" demanded the chef.

"Nothing," calmly answered the diner, "I just don't have a spoon."

❤The modern man comes home from work and greets his wife with: "Hi - ya, honey, what's thawing?"

❤*Waitress:* "This is your fifth cup, sir; you must like coffee!"

Diner: "I do; that's why I am willing to drink all this water to get a little of it."

❤No matter how little you expect from a TV dinner, you will always be disappointed.

❤A salad bar is where people go to exchange germs.

❤"Darling," said the bride as she put dinner on the table, "this is my first roast turkey."

"Marvelous! And it looks as if you've stuffed it well, too."

"Stuffed it? Why this one wasn't hollow."

❤The young minister sitting down to dinner was asked by his wife to say grace. He opened the casserole dish she had prepared from a new French recipe book and an uncounted number of refrigerator left-overs.

"Well, I don't know," he said, "it seems to me I've blessed all this stuff before."

❤Joey Adams tells of a fisherman who met a friend on his way home.

"Where are you going with that lobster under your arm?" the angler asked.

"I'm taking him home to dinner."

Just then the lobster piped up: "I've already had my dinner; how about a movie?"

❤"Good heavens, Mr. Druggist, I'm poisoned!" the customer shouted. "It must have been the sandwiches my wife gave me."

"Yes, that's it," agreed the pharmacist. "You're taking a chance every time you eat a sandwich that isn't prepared by a registered pharmacist."

❤Madison Avenue is where they spend massive amounts of money trying to sell products that "taste like home-made" to a generation that doesn't know what "home-made" tastes like.

❤A recession is when we're faced with still another problem: What wine goes with nothing?

❤A typical banquet is where the red is always served at room temperature. Sometimes it's the wine. Sometimes it's the strawberry ice cream.

Definitions

❤A poet is a person who tells the truth about something that never happened.

❤A pessimist is a person who thinks the world is going to the dogs because he isn't running it.

❤Dignity is the capacity to hold back on the tongue what never should have been on the mind in the first place.

❤Compliment: A remark that need not be true to be gratefully received.

❤To the pessimist, O is the last letter in zero, but to the optimist it's the first letter in opportunity.

❤A psychiatrist is a person who doesn't have to worry so long as others do.

❤A pessimist is a person who knows he isn't as smart as those who want to borrow money from him tell him he is.

❤Neurotic — A person who thinks you mean it when you ask how he is.

❤"Father," said a small boy, "what is a demagogue?"
"A demagogue, my son, is a man who can rock the boat himself and persuade everybody else that there is a terrible storm at sea."

❤Diplomats believe many powwows keep the world from going to the bowwows.

❤A specialist is someone who has focused all of his ignorance onto one subject.

❤Nostalgia is when you live life in the past lane.

❤A hurricane is when they predict high winds and scattered landscape.

❤A hurricane is when the garage door stays in place but the house goes up.

❤Chamber of Commerce executive: A man who will never admit he's seen better days.

❤Let me try to explain this in terms people can understand. Inflation is when everyone charges what the TV repairman charges.

❤An ulcer is when you mix business with pressure.

❤A radio announcer is a man who tries to get the commercial in before the listener can change stations.

❤Tourist — A man in sport clothes with a head cold.

❤Whenever I hear that some bit of information comes from a reliable source, I always think of the derivation of the word "reliable". It consists of "liable" as in being able to lie – and "re" as in time and time again.

❤A bargain is something you cannot use at a price you cannot resist.

❤Mixed emotions is having your picture appear on the cover of *Time* – and it's the one from your passport.

❤A consultant is like an usher in an X-rated movie. He helps you to get the best view of things.

❤A coed is a girl who didn't get her man in high school.

❤An optimist is a person who saves the pictures in the seed catalog to compare them with the flowers and vegetables he grows.

Health & Fitness

❤You may be able to make some people think you are younger than you are, but you can't fool a hamburger, just before bedtime.

❤"You are very run down," said the doctor to his patient. "I suggest you lay off golf for a while and get a good day in now and then at the office."

❤Patient: "How can I ever repay you for your kindness to me?"

Doctor: "By check, money order, or cash."

❤It was so tough for Bill to get up in the morning that he went to see his doctor, who fixed him up with some pills to cure him of drowsiness. Bill took a pill that night, slept well, and was wide awake before he heard the alarm go off. He dressed and ate breakfast leisurely. Later he told the boss:

"I didn't have a bit of trouble getting up this morning."

"That's fine," the boss said, "but where were you yesterday?"

❤Scientists have just discovered why the new generation is taller than any previous generation in history. It's because the TV channel selector is always at the top of the set.

❤A friend of mine stopped smoking, drinking, over-eating and chasing women – all at the same time. It was a lovely funeral.

❤"Laugh and grow fat" seems like fine advice — until you try it and find that it works.

❤Jogging is what you take up for your health's sake and give up for your body's sake.

❤I'm not really into exercise. To me, a barbell is something you ring when you want another drink.

❤After a month on a new diet, Mrs. Jones was asked what she weighed. "One hundred and plenty," she replied.

❤Let him who doesn't wish to die yet diet.

❤Diet: Something to take the starch out of you.

❤Doctors advise walking for health, but I've yet to see a mailman who looked as if he could whip a truckdriver.

❤There may be a destiny that shapes our ends, but our middles are of our own chewsing.

❤"If you insist on smoking in bed, the ashes you drop on the floor may be your own."

❤I just joined that new organization of fat people who couldn't care less. Their motto is: A WAIST IS A TERRIBLE THING TO MIND.

His wife says it's just like being married to Santa Claus.
Every night he comes home with a bag on.

Hodge-Podge

♥Betsy Ross created the first flag. She put in blue because of the mighty oceans that beat against our shores. She put in white because of the purity of our highest aspirations. She put in red because she pricked her fingers a lot.

♥There is a girl on my street with a lot health problems. You have to feel sorry for anybody who has her appendix taken out – every nine months.

♥It was so embarrassing. She had one of those bathing suits with built in foam rubber, went swimming – and absorbed the pool.

❤Excuse me sir but I notice you're beginning to hesitate. That's a good sign. It means your brain is trying to make contact with your mouth.

❤Conceited? His idea of being unfaithful is turning away from a mirror.

❤He puts his foot in his mouth so often, his favorite flavor is toe.

❤His record is one out of two. And that's just applying his spray deodorant.

❤I wouldn't call him a liar. Let's just say he lives on the wrong side of the facts.

❤I wasn't swearing, I was just quoting so and so.

❤Never give up, you'll never know how close you come to success. Look at the inventor of Preparation G.

❤Original? They just named a carbon paper after him.

❤I won't say what she looked like but when I wanted to get romantic, the first thing I took off was my glasses.

❤I made a list of things I could do without if prices get too high and liquor is on the list. Right after air.

❤I can tell I'm getting old. I don't even fall down as fast as I used to.

❤Santa Claus spends a whole year trying to find out who was naughty and nice. Any secretary could tell him in a minute.

❤I just got my first pair of bifocals and it's quite an experience. It's the first time I ever fell up the stairs.

❤I've always had bad luck. I once invested $10,000 in a

prized dog for breeding purposes. Got him home and found out he barked with a lisp.

❤I wouldn't say she talks a lot but if she ever ate her words, she would put on 50 lbs.

❤Terrible things always happen to me. I once had a goldfish that ran away from home.

❤I wouldn't say he's dull but when he walks through his garden, his geraniums yawn.

❤I keep having this terrible dream. I'm in a leaking row boat but not really worried because the ship is on the way – the *Titantic*.

❤Our local fire department has its first woman member and she's doing fine – once she made it clear that the only thing she was going to put out was fires.

❤Is there anything more embarrassing than coming out of your Memory Improvement class and forgetting where you parked the car?

❤It's amazing. Yesterday we went out and her slip was showing. What makes it so amazing, she was wearing slacks!

❤I happen to be allergic to bikinis. Everytime I see one my eyes break out.

❤I don't ask for much out of life. Just once I'd like to ride in a limousine and it isn't following a hearse.

❤My car and I have the same bad habits. We both drink, smoke, and can't get started in the morning.

❤The latest trend in psychology is for people to be as-sertive. Say precisely what you think when you think it and it will completely change the shape of your personality. I agree. I was in a bar once and I said to this truck driver precisely what I thought when I thought it – and it did change the shape of my personality, starting with my nose.

❤Did you ever get out of the shower, look at yourself in a full length mirror – and want to send your birthday suit back for alterations?

❤Age changes your perspective on so many things. When I was young, I thought a man of 50 might be ready for the grave. Now that I'm 50 – I'm sure of it.

❤40 is when you start to go downhill. 50 is when you do it on a skateboard.

❤Cheap? The only time I've ever seen him pick up a tab was on a beer can.

❤I hate to take naps. Waking up once a day is bad enough.

❤Conceited? He thinks they wrote a song about him: THE BEST THINGS IN LIFE ARE ME.

❤I'm not going to say he cheats at golf. Let's just put it this way: Last year he wore out three clubs and six erasers.

❤I've come to the conclusion that my problem in life isn't any lack of intelligence – it's just plain forgetfulness. That must be it – because when I was eighteen, I knew everything!

❤In conclusion, let me end this session with one sobering thought; It's ten o'clock. Do you know where your Treasurer is?

❤Do you ever get the feeling you've been voted The

I don't have a very strong personality. Last week all my friends, neighbors and relatives got together to give me a birthday party and I didn't show up. Nobody noticed.

Man of the Rear?

♥Football is a great sport, but you do have to admit that the people who play it are confused. Very confused. What other game has twelve gorgeous pompom girls standing on the sidelines and who do the players pat on the fanny? Each other!

♥I'd give my right arm to be ambidextrous.

♥Being 55 is like driving 55 – everybody seems to pass you.

♥It pays to be courteous. For instance, this morning I gave my place on a supermarket checkout line to a guy with only two items – a note and a gun.

❤I'll never forget the time I started going with the Class valedictorian. Had an I.Q. of 162 and she never let me forget it. She sent me torrid, passionate love letters – with footnotes.

❤If you're a born loser, you were born at the right time.

❤I believe that we must all fight against temptation – but not hard enough to discourage it.

❤(UNUSUAL OUTFIT): That's what I call a class action suit. It has a lot more action than class.

❤That old legend is true. If you tell anyone they have a shape like an elephant – they'll never forget it.

❤(INTERRUPTER) Sir, has it ever occurred to you that, on the road to success, your mouth might be a pothole.

❤The true measure of a man's character is what he says when he drops a ten pound Bible on his foot.

❤I was born on a farm and I guess it shows. To this day, I still put on my coat to go to the bathroom.

❤LAWYER: I won't comment on his practice but when it comes to serving his clients, he believes in leaving no stone unturned. Which is fortunate, because that's where he finds a lot of his clients.

❤Let's not say he's lazy. Let's just say that when it comes to burning ambition, he could be classified as flame retardant.

❤On New Year's Eve, at the stroke of midnight, you are supposed to lean over and kiss the one you love most. With some, it's a husband. With others, it a wife. With still others, it's a mirror.

For Father's Day, my kids always give me a shaving lotion called English Leather. Which is very appropriate. To them I've always smelled like a wallet.

Holidays

❤Christmas is that magic time when the year runs out, the neighbors run in, the batteries run down and the bills run up.

❤Christmas is when you tip the parking lot attendant, you tip the maitre d', you tip the doorman, you tip the paper boy. It's called – Season's Greasings.

❤As we celebrate yet another Valentine's Day, I have only one question: If we're living in such a sexually permissive society – how come it's so hard to get permission?

❤The trouble with Thanksgiving dinners is – you eat one and a month later you're hungry again.

❤In 1984, Father's Day presents a new kind of challenge. What do you give to the man who needs everything?

❤Every year I do the same thing on Halloween. I go over to my sister's house and scare the daylights out of my brother-in-law. I dress up as a job.

❤Thanksgiving is the traditional time for families to come together and revive old memories. In fact, my in-laws said it seemed like just yesterday that they were over at our house – eating, drinking, enjoying the good life – and it really brought tears to my eyes – because it was just yesterday that they were over at our house – eating, drinking…

❤We always observed a very traditional holiday. Every Christmas Eve we'd be visited by a jolly gent carrying something over his shoulder that was loaded. It was a cop with father.

Law

❤Thirty days hath September, April, June, and my uncle for taking bets on the horses.

❤He'd driven for miles across sparsely settled territory before he finally came to a little town boasting a hotel of sorts. Sitting down for supper at the single table at which everyone was served, the motorist complained about the condition of the roller towel he had been forced to use. "Besides," he wound up, "roller towels have been prohibited by law for years!"

"Sure," replied the proprietor. "I know about that law. But I had that towel a-hanging there before they passed it."

❤When the defendant's name was called in court, to everyone's amazement, he stood up in the jury box. "What are you doing there?" barked the clerk.

"I was called to serve on the jury," came the meek reply. "But you must have known," the clerk snapped, "that you couldn't sit on a jury and judge your own case."

"Well, I suppose not," the defendant admitted. "I did think it was a bit of luck."

❤A householder excitedly reported to the police that he had been struck down in the dark outside his back door by an unknown assailant.

A policeman was sent to the scene of the crime and soon returned to headquarters with a lump on his forehead and a glum look on his face.

"I solved the case," he muttered.

"Fast work," his superior complimented him. "How did you accomplish it?"

The young cop explained, "I stepped on the rake, too."

❤*Policeman:* "Hey you, didn't you hear me say, 'Pull over'?"

Driver: "Oh, I thought you said, 'Good morning, Mayor!'"

Policeman: "It is a nice morning, isn't it?"

❤The application blank for a new driver's license held the question, "Have you ever been arrested?" The applicant put down "No."

The next question was, "Why?" The applicant put down, "Never been caught."

❤Two friends met who hadn't seen each other for some time. One was on crutches. "Hello," said the other man. "What's the matter?" "Streetcar accident," said the man on crutches. "When did it happen?" "About six weeks ago." "And you still have to use crutches?" "Well, my doctor says I could get along without them, but my lawyer says I can't."

❤An anonymous New York taxpayer sent a letter to the State Comptroller's office in Albany, saying that he had cheated on his income tax ten years ago, and had not been able to get a good night's sleep since. He enclosed twenty-five dollars, and added, "If I still can't sleep, I'll send the balance."

♥One attorney wrote to another, "Sir: I regret to inform you that there is danger of an agreement between our respective clients."

♥But I think we should all be very grateful to lawyers. Lawyers are the people who get us out of all the trouble we never would have gotten into if it hadn't been for lawyers.

♥I have a great lawyer. Specializes in negligence. Three times this week he couldn't find my file.

♥The policeman stopped the man going down the street clad only in a barrel. "Are you a poker player?" the voice of the law demanded.

"No, I'm not," the culprit replied, "but I just left a group of fellows who are."

♥"So, Lefty, not content with stealing five thousand dollars in cash, you went back and took a couple of watches, six diamond rings, and a pearl necklace?"

"Yes, Your Honor. I remembered that money alone doesn't bring happiness."

♥A woman was called for jury duty, but refused to serve because she didn't believe in capital punishment. Trying to persuade her, the judge explained: "This is only a case where a wife is suing her husband because she gave him $1,000 to pay down on a fur coat, and he lost the money in a poker game."

Thereupon the woman said: "I'll serve. I could be wrong about capital punishment."

❤The traffic officer ordered the motorist to pull up to the curb and produce his driver's license. "I don't understand this, officer," the motorist protested. "I haven't done anything wrong." "No, you haven't," the officer replied. "But you were driving so carefully, I thought you might not have your driver's license."

❤When a traffic officer stops you, he either gives you a ticket or sells you one.

❤An honest city is one where no one knows a rich policeman.

There is justice in this world. Yesterday the fella stealing my tires was run over by the fella stealing my car.

Love & Marriage

❤Last fall she had dismissed her boy friend, saying she couldn't think of marrying him until he had saved a few thousand dollars. Came spring…a gorgeous night and a full moon. Again – how much had he saved?
"About thirty-five dollars," he said.
"Well," said Joan, with a blush, "that's enough."

❤Love is like eating a mushroom. By the time you know whether it's the real thing, it's too late.

❤Advice to young men in love: Never tell the girl you are unworthy of her. Let that come later as a complete surprise.

❤When a boy holds a girl's hand at the movies, he may be doing it to keep her from eating his popcorn.

❤Most husbands want a wife they can love, honor and display.

❤Home is a place where a man is free to say anything he pleases, because no one will pay the slightest attention to him.

❤Before I married Maggie dear I was her pumpkin pie, her precious peach, her honey lamb, the apple of her eye. But after years of married life this thought I pause to utter; those fancy names are gone, and now I'm just her bread and butter.

❤Two men were talking about how they came to get married. "Where did you meet your wife?" asked one.
"In a travel bureau," came the reply.
"Were you going somewhere?"
"No, but she was looking for a vacation and I was the last resort."

❤A girl considers college a success if she quits to get married.

❤"You should marry and let a wife share your life."
"Not for me. Some shareholders become directors."

❤What the average woman wants is a great big strong man who can be wrapped around her finger.

❤Two women were talking. One remarked, "Last week I advertised in the paper for a husband."
The other asked. "Get any replies?"
"Hundreds of them. And they were all the same. They all said, 'You can have mine.'"

❤ What makes you think your wife is getting tired of you?"
"Every day this week she has wrapped my lunch in a road map!"

❤The best thing for newly-weds to feather their nest with is plenty of cash down.

❤"Those new people across the street seem very devoted. Every time he goes out he kisses her, and he goes on throwing kisses all the way down the street. Albert, why don't you do that?"
"Me? I don't even know her."

❤Overheard on the beach: "Mother, may I go for a

swim?"

"Certainly not, my dear, it's far too deep."

"But Daddy is swimming."

"Yes, dear, but he's insured."

❤*Husband to wife:* "What do you say we take this money we've been saving toward a new car and blow it on a movie?"

❤Married life: First you carry the bride over the threshold then she puts her foot down.

❤Of all the labor-saving devices invented for women none has ever been so popular as a husband with money.

❤Woman to her husband: "When I want your opinion, I'll give it to you."

❤Any married man who agrees with his wife can have his own way.

❤"They say brunettes have sweeter dispositions than redheads."

"That's a lot of hooey. My wife's been both and I can't see any difference."

❤"Has your husband changed much in the years you've been married?" asked one wife of another.

"No," was the reply, "but he thinks he has. He's always talking about what a fool he used to be."

❤I cured my wife of her antique craze! I just made her a birthday present of a 1923 model automobile.

❤A man wanted to buy a riding horse for his wife and was trying one out. Noticing that the horse required a firm hand and constant watching, he asked, "Do you think this is a suitable horse for a woman?"

The owner of the horse was a reasonably honest man, so he answered carefully: "Well, I think a woman could handle the horse, but I wouldn't want to be the husband of the woman who could do it!"

❤Mr. Jones and his family had just returned from their vacation. "Did you enjoy your vacation trip?" asked a neighbor of Mr. Jones.

"Very much," Mr. Jones replied.

"My wife did all the driving."

"Then you had a chance to enjoy the scenery."

"Yes, indeed," said Mr. Jones.

"All I had to do was to hold the wheel."

❤"Jane," moaned her husband, "you promised you wouldn't buy another new dress. What made you do it?"

"Dear," she replied, "the devil tempted me."

"Why didn't you say: 'Get thee behind me, Satan?'" her husband inquired.

"I did," the woman replied, sweetly, "and then he whispered over my shoulder: 'My dear, it fits you just beautifully at the back.'"

❤"They tell me your wife is outspoken."

"By whom?"

❤*Client:* "Do you think you can make a good portrait of my wife?" *Artist:* "My friend, I can make it so life-like that you'll jump every time you see it."

❤"Jack, dear," said the bride, "let us try to make the people believe we've been married a long time."

"All right, honey," came the reply, "but do you think you can carry both suitcases?"

❤Marriage is when two people who can't get too much of each other do.

❤We seem to be living in the age of instant marriage – love at first sight and divorce at first fight.

❤What can you really say about the divorce rate? Statistics now show that people are marrying more, but enduring it less.

❤There are always two sides to every divorce – both wrong.

❤Her idea of gourmet cooking is adding oregano to a

Warning: If your wife wants to learn to drive, don't stand in her way.

TV dinner.

❤My wife and I are always ready to leave for a party at the same time, and it's all because I have a system. The first time she says, "I'm ready" – I start to shave.

❤Living happily ever after depends in part on what you're after.

❤When a pensive little thing gets married, she often becomes an expensive little thing.

❤When they asked the movie actress how long she had been married, she said, "This time or all together?"

❤*Judge:* "I think you might as well give your husband a divorce."

   Wife: "What! I lived with this bum for twenty years and now I should make him happy?"

❤*Doctor:* "Now, madam, place this thermometer between your teeth and keep your lips closed for five minutes."

   Husband (aside to doctor): "What will you take for that gadget, Doc?"

❤"Is it possible for a man to make a fool of himself without knowing it?"

   "Not if he has a wife."

❤To be unhappily married requires a good income and to be incompatible a couple must be rich.

❤"Last week a grain of sand got into my wife's eye, and she had to go to a doctor. It cost me $40."

   "That's nothing. Last week a fur coat got into my wife's eye, and it cost me $4,000."

❤I once asked my grandpa why a man is not allowed to

have more than one wife, and he said: "Son when you're older you'll realize that the law protects those who are incapable of protecting themselves."

❤*Husband:* "It must be time to get up."

Wife: "Why?"

Husband: "The baby's fallen asleep."

❤She had only three requirements for a husband – money, wealth and property.

❤Wife to husband: "All right, I admit I like to spend money... but name one other extravagance."

Medical

❤My doctor just divorced his wife and I don't blame him. Every night, just before they got into bed, she gave him an apple.

❤My neighbor is a hypochondriac. He joined a golf club just to be able to find a doctor on Wednesday afternoons!

❤At my age, an acid trip is going down to the corner for a roll of Tums.

❤A doctor is someone who can put a stethoscope against Raquel Welch's chest and hear his heart beat.

❤I'll say one thing for our local doctor – he has never violated his oath. The oath he took 22 years ago when he swore to become a millionaire.

❤A lot of people are confused about the difference between generic and brand names, but it's really rather simple. A generic name would be Vitamin E. The brand name would be Honeymoon Helper.

❤He's a very hip doctor – the only psychiatrist I know with a water couch.

❤You know what worries me? Doctors are now saying that smoking is four times worse than they originally thought – and what they originally thought is that it would kill you.

♥I go to a real sneaky doctor. Yesterday afternoon he said he couldn't see me because he had to do something about an iron deficiency. Then he left for the golf course.

♥There are three reasons why golf caddies live longer than any other category of worker: They get plenty of fresh air; and if there's an emergency – there's always a doctor nearby.

♥Personally, I get all the exercise I need by subscribing to forty different magazines. Every time one of them is delivered, I open it up, then I bend down to the floor to pick up the subscription card that falls out.

♥Yesterday I went to a doctor. I told him I didn't seem to have as much energy as I used to. He said I was having a mid-life meltdown.

♥It's a funny thing about doctors: When you try to make an appointment with a doctor, they float like a butterfly. But when you get their bill, they sting like a bee.

♥The problem of middle-aged runners can be summed up by this exchange during a recent marathon. One said, "I don't want to brag, but I've got the body of a 20 year old ." And the other said, "Give it back. You're getting it all wrinkled."

♥We're living in an age of medical specialists. Nowadays what four out of five doctors recommend is another doctor.

♥I go to what's called a family physician. He treats mine and I support his.

❤Our son had to drop out of medical school. Flunked Second Opinion.

❤I try to be honest in all things. When I go to a doctor and he says, "Tell me where it hurts," – I point to my wallet.

❤I'm a little depressed over what happened at my annual physical check-up. According to my height and weight chart – I should be a Toyota.

❤Women should register for the draft because they're much healthier than men. When they go down for their physical, you never hear them coughing.

❤If you're my age, watching the Miss America pageant is like going to a travelogue. It's nice to see so many places you ain't never going to get to in person.

❤I've reached the age where every time I see an antique, I remember putting something like it out with the trash.

❤You know you're getting along when people hold the door open for you – and have to wait until you get there.

❤I've reached that stage in life where I know where its at – but it's a little further than I want to go.

❤I figure there are two reasons for worrying about tomorrow – yesterday and today.

❤I never knew my uncle was a hyprochondriac until a doctor told him he was in perfect health – and he asked for a second opinion.

❤We'll be having our annual credit card vacation. For the next few weeks we'll be getting away from it all.

And then, for the next few months, they'll be getting it all away from us.

❤I never really believed retired people were eating dog food until that poll came out. The one that lists their four favorite forms of recreation: Golf, television, shuffleboard and chasing cars.

❤Doctors really have it made. First he told me to give up wine, women and song – then he prescribed something for depression.

❤My doctor has an interesting approach to medicine. I opened my wallet and he said "ah"'

❤A recent study lists the three major causes of heart attacks: cholesterol, overweight and husbands coming home early.

❤We knew he had a problem when his doctor gave him a prescription to help him stop drinking and he used it as a coaster.

❤It pays to check into the educational background of your physician. For instance, beware of any doctor whose major was accounting and whose minor was medicine.

❤Studies now show that, on average, anyone who runs ten miles a day, every day, in good weather and bad, in the blazing summer heat and in the frigid winter cold – will live to the age of 82. And even if they *don't* live till 82 – they'll *look* 82.

❤If you're a doctor, you can expect to face constant challenges, frustration, adversity and yes, even heartbreak. So much for golf, now let's talk about medicine.

❤Modern medical treatment is based on three simple letters: T.L.C. Takes Lotsa Cash!

❤I went to the doctor and told him I had a pain in my little finger. He told me to come back when I had something more expensive.

❤Crime is everywhere. I went into surgery last month – and some guy in a mask pulled a knife on me.

❤After waiting hours in a crowded doctor's office, one patient stood up to go. He said, "Well, I guess I'll just go home and die a natural death."

Nobody can be sure what long-term effect nuclear radiation has on people. For instance, my Uncle Willie worked in a nuclear power plant for 15 years, put in for early retirement and just last week started a second career in Portland, Maine – as a lighthouse.

❤As the Chinese doctor said to his patient, "Long time no fee."

❤A minor operation is one that was performed on the other fellow.

❤*Teacher:* "Are you doing anything for your cold?"
Boy: "I sneeze when it wants me to."

❤*Margie:* "Why do you keep stamps in the medicine cabinet?"
Freddie: "Why not? I buy them at the drug store."

❤Kids today are so much more sophisticated than we were. When I was a kid I was really naive. For instance, every time I played Doctor with the girl next door – I was a podiatrist.

Miscellaneous

❤A man walking down the street on a dark night passed an alley. Two thugs jumped on him, and though he put up a terrific fight they got him down. After they searched him, they were amazed at the small sum of money they found in his pockets. "You mean you put up that fight for sixty-seven cents?" they asked.

"Shucks, no," answered the victim, "I thought you were after the $500 in my shoe."

❤A man entered a meeting with a piece of paper in his hand, and said, "This is a list of all the men I can whip."

A husky, broad-shouldered boiler-maker exclaimed, "Is my name on there?"

The man said, "Yes."

"Well," bellowed the husky, "you can't whip me!"

"Are you sure?" asked the challenger.

"Bet yer life I'm sure!" yelled the fellow.

"Okay, then," replied the man, "I'll take your name off the list."

❤"Hear no evil, see no evil, speak no evil," and you'll certainly be a dull companion.

❤Then there was the man who appeared in a newspaper office to place an ad offering $500 for the return of his wife's pet cat.

"That's an awful price for a cat," the clerk commented. "Not for this one," the man snapped. "I drowned it."

❤Prejudice is an unwillingness to be confused with facts.

❤"What funny names those Korean towns have," remarked a man from Schenectady, as he read a Poughkeepsie newspaper while on his way to Hackensack.

❤Egotism is the art of seeing things in yourself that others cannot.

❤Jean says she never saw a vitamin, but she's sure she'd rather C than B_1.

❤The greatest disadvantage in life is to have too many advantages.

❤Procrastination is the thief of time — and so is every other big word.

❤An antique collector, passing through a small village, stopped to watch an old man chopping wood with an ancient ax.

"That's a mighty old ax you have there," remarked the collector.

"Yes," said the villager, "it once belonged to George Washington."

"Not really!" gasped the collector. "It certainly stood up well."

"Of course," admitted the old man, "it's had three new handles and two new heads."

❤*Tenant:* "The people upstairs are very annoying. Last night they stamped and banged on the floor after midnight."

Landlord: "Did they awaken you?"

Tenant: "No. As it happened, I was still up practicing on my tuba."

❤The first screw that gets loose in a person's head is the one that controls the tongue.

❤The man who says he's a 100 per cent American probable made the appraisal himself.

❤Two hoboes headed south of town and settled down on the fairways of a country club to eat their food. Along came one of the members. "Get out of here, you bums," he shouted. "This is private property! It costs hundreds of dollars to belong to this club!"

 "OK, OK," said one of the bums, pulling himself up to his full height and brushing the crumbs away. "But let me warn you, this is no way to get new members."

❤Kindness is one thing you can't give away. It always comes back.

❤It's always fair weather when a Californian meets a native of Florida.

❤He's writing his alibiography.

❤The driver of a sightseeing bus who was describing a Southern battlefield of the Civil War told of many Southern victories. Finally a Northerner in the car asked him, "Didn't the North win any battles in the Civil War?"

 The Southern driver said, "No sir, Mister. They ain't won a battle and they ain't going to as long as I'm drivin' this sightseeing bus."

❤*Motorist:* "I ran over your cat and I want to replace him."

Housewife: "Well, get busy. There's a mouse in the pantry."

❤A fool and his money are invited places.

❤An intoxicated person fell out of a seven story window and landed in the street without any apparent harm.

A crowd gathered and a policeman rushed up and said, "What happened?"

"I don't know," said the intoxicated man. "I just got here myself."

❤The despondent gentleman emerged from his club and climbed stiffly into a limousine.

"Where to, sir?" asked the chauffeur respectfully.

"Drive off a cliff, James. I'm committing suicide."

❤Despite what the cartoonists make him look like, Uncle Sam is a gentleman with a very large waste.

❤A mountaineer took a trip to New York City – his first to a large city. On his return, a friend asked him how he liked New York.

"Well," said Zeke, "to tell the truth, I never did get to see the town — there was so much going on around the depot."

❤Two can live as cheaply as one, and they generally have to.

❤Life is a constant struggle to keep up appearances and keep down expenses.

❤Some people are like buttons – continually popping

off.

❤In September most of the forks return from the summer resorts for a greatly-needed rest.

❤Weatherman's description of his infant son: Dry and sunny, but subject to change.

❤Think how surprised a mink must be who goes to sleep in a Wisconsin marsh and wakes up in the Metropolitan opera house.

❤A finance agency was having trouble collecting from a man named Jones – Finally, they wrote him: "Dear Mr. Jones: What would your neighbors think if we came to your town and repossessed your car?"

A week later they received their letter back. Scrawled on it was this message: "I took the matter up with my neighbors and they think it would be a lousy trick. Sincerely, L. Jones."

❤Sometimes we think the television hero is the one who sits through the program.

❤An army travels on its stomach, but some individuals travel on their gall.

❤There is one advantage of poor handwriting. It covers up a lot of mistakes in spelling.

❤When you have trouble, you learn which friends have been waiting with a paddle to find you bent over.

❤ An Eskimo is the only person who sits on top of the world, and he lives in an igloo and eats blubber.

❤A man who owns a summer cottage on a lake may not have a good time during the summer season, but the chances are dozens of his friends who visit him do.

They laughed when I spoke to the waiter in French — they didn't I know I told him to give the check to the other guy.

♥Some people think they have dynamic personalities because they're always exploding.

♥If you can't see the forest for the trees, you may be in the desert.

♥Somethings don't make sense – like a coffin with a life-time guarantee.

♥My family lives in a very tough neighborhood. Very tough. For instance, my Cousin Eddie is the oldest living graduate of his class. Now that may not sound like much to you, but he graduated last June!

♥You don't have to be a cannibal to get fed up with

people.

❤They say that even garbage can be made into gasoline. Why not? It's already being made into movies, books and TV shows.

❤Have you ever stopped to ask yourself, what would the snail darter do if we were endangered?

❤They just built a roller coaster for people that live in San Francisco. It's level.

❤If at first you don't succeed – deny you were trying.

❤The best time to plant an oak tree is thirty years ago.

❤Going to a nude beach can be a very educational experience. It teaches you why people wear clothes.

❤We don't live in a logical world. If we did, men would ride sidesaddle.

❤What I like about a vacation is, it fills so much of your year. If you take your vacation in August – you get your slides back in September; your bills back in October; your health back in November; and your luggage back in December.

❤A good deal of the room at the top is made by men who have gone to sleep there, and fallen off.

❤When it comes to giving, some people stop at nothing.

❤It's so dry in San Francisco, it's the first time I ever saw a tree go up to a dog.

❤Spring is God's way of saying: "One more time."

❤It's kinda sad to know there are 24 hours in a day and only one of them is referred to as the Happy Hour.

❤Service station washrooms are where it takes you fifteen minutes just to clean the soap.

❤A tradition is what you have when you're too lazy to think up something new.

❤There are no simple answers. Simple answerers, yes.

❤As nervous as a man in a waterbed with sharp toenails.

❤Bad manners are like bad teeth. Nobody knows you have them if you keep your mouth shut.

❤But it was a very civic-minded community. Once a week they held a bingo game and all the proceeds went to fight gambling.

❤I live in one of those neighborhoods where everybody

Summer is the time when the weather gets too hot to cook and the relatives come to visit you.

keeps their hubcaps in the trunk.

❤The best way to check the "life of the party" is to let him pick up the check.

❤You know you have a hangover when you apply your underarm spray and miss.

❤Drama pages are "a sort of paper coffin where dead plays are buried."

❤Critic: "A string quartet played Brahms last evening. Brahms lost."

❤Self-confident? This man is without a doubt – without a doubt.

❤"Did anyone in your family ever make a brilliant marriage?"

"Only my husband."

❤The sergeant was drilling raw recruits. It was a hectic job. Finally he noticed one man alone was out of step.
"Do you know, soldier," he said sarcastically, "that they're all out of step except you?"
"Well," replied the rookie, "you're in charge – you tell 'em!"

❤ *Neighbor:* "You say your son is only four, and he can spell his name backwards? What's his name?"
Proud parent: "Otto."

❤"Hilda, what on earth are you taking those avocado peels home for?"
"Well, ma'am, they make my garbage look so stylish."

❤"See this jewelry?" said the sorority pledge. "It once belonged to a millionaire."

"Gosh," gasped an impressed sister, "what was his name?"

"Woolworth," the pledge replied.

❤Rich? Who else do you know with a Gucci Christmas tree?

❤Nowadays every toy is electronic. My five year old is the envy of every kid on the block. For Christmas we gave him a battery-operated battery.

❤Worry is like a rocking chair – gives you something to do, but doesn't get you anywhere,

Money

❤You can't measure a person's happiness by the amount of money he has. A man with ten million dollars may be no happier than one who has only nine million.

❤Let no one tell you that a fool and his money are soon parted. A fool rarely has any money.

❤Some persons believe you don't need principle to live if you have principal.

❤A living wage is a little more than you are making now.

❤For demanding money with threats a man was imprisoned. Will the income tax collector please note.

❤When it comes to tax reductions, never do so many wait so anxiously for so little for so long.

❤Success nowadays is making more money to pay the taxes you wouldn't be paying if you hadn't made so much money already.

❤Sure money talks, but nowadays you can't hold on to it long enough to start a conversation.

❤An optimist thinks he is as smart as the fellow who wants to borrow $10 from him tells him he is.

❤What we'd like to know is where the people who live beyond their incomes get the money with which to live beyond their incomes.

❤It is pitiful to see someone squander money and know you can't help him.

❤He cut quite a figure among his friends, but his bank account looked like zero.

❤The beauty about the vacation season is that if you don't pay your bills your creditors think you are away.

❤A timely slogan: Work and save, young man, and some day you'll have enough to divide with those who don't.

❤People who say money can't buy happiness don't know what happiness is.

❤Don't knock the rich. When was the last time you were hired by anyone poor?

❤I go to a typical neighborhood bank. There are always four people standing behind the counter. One is called *Clara Jones* – and the rest are called *Next Window*.

❤I think someone just asked our local banker for a mortgage. I'd know his laugh anywhere.

❤Have you noticed how people in Florida are always bragging about the water and the weather. For instance, the last time I went to Miami Beach, the bellboy carried four suitcases up to my room. So I gave him a quarter tip – and as he was leaving, I could hear him talking about the sun and the beach.

❤There's nothing complicated about the meatpacking business. Ranchers sell beef by the head; middlemen sell it by the side; and consumers get it in the end.

❤We're living in strange times – when luxury is being able to afford necessities.

❤And now for our helpful hint of the week: The next

Next to being shot at and missed, nothing is quite as satisfying as an income tax refund.

time you see a dollar bill on the street, pick it up. There might be something valuable underneath.

❤Flowers are always very popular on Mother's Day. I once asked a florist to explain why roses cost $35 a dozen. He said, "Well, it requires an enormous amount of care, know-how and manure." I asked, "To grow the roses?" He said, "No. To explain why they cost $35 a dozen."

❤New York is such a friendly town. The very first day I was there I shook five hands. Three were in my hotel and two were in my pocket.

❤I don't want to brag, but when I go, I'm going to be

leaving my kids something that comes to $150,000. The mortgage.

❤I'm a big fan of movies. For only $6, movies can buy you more sex, violence, mystery, intrigue and surprises than anything else I know – with the possible exception of a marriage license.

❤"Two can live as cheaply as one." *The old proverb.* "Two must live as cheaply as one." *The new Social Security.*

❤The new economic program has finally got us all moving in the same direction. The Army, Navy, Marines and Air Force are going to get more guns and so are the poor.

❤I went to Wall Street last week. Visited the Tomb of the Unknown Optimist.

❤On pay day, we always have a very special, elegant and expensive dinner, starting off with soup – Cream of Salary.

❤Rich? Last year he took a cab when he went to the hospital for an operation – and told the driver to wait.

❤Old? He remembers when Karl Malden carried cash.

❤The important thing to remember about exercise is to start slow – and then gradually taper off.

❤This is the time of the year when people start going places where they pay $200 a day to experience the same kind of heat they were complaining about in August.

❤We deal with a very strict bank. It's called the First Savings and Lien.

❤I have a real problem with teenagers studying economics. I mean, what could a high school teacher possibly know about money?

❤Our life expectancy keeps going up. According to the latest statistics, average Americans will now live seven years past the time when their money runs out.

❤I go to one of those income tax services that speak up for you if your return is audited. What they say is: "Who?"

One Liners

❤Success has always operated on the serve-yourself plan.

❤There is a difference between having an aim in life and just shooting at random.

❤The man who sings his own praise invariably sings a solo unaccompanied.

❤The rainy days for which a person saves usually come during his vacation.

❤In life, as in a mirror, you never get more out than you put in.

❤Those who try to do something and fail are infinitely better than those who try to do nothing and succeed.

❤The best cure for a sluggish mind is to disturb its routine.

❤THE *TITANIC* WAS A ONE-LINER.

❤All genuine progress results from finding new facts.

❤I have a great system for breaking even in Las Vegas. I don't go.

❤Fanaticism should be practised in moderation.

❤To be the man of the hour, first learn to make every minute count.

❤To be frank is to tell the truth about anything that won't hurt you.

❤When you help someone up hill, you find yourself

closer to the top.

❤God made everything out of nothing but man seems to make nothing out of everything.

❤Always do right. This will gratify some people, and astonish the rest.

❤You never get ahead of anyone as long as you are trying to get even.

❤When you tell your troubles to some one else, you should be willing to listen to theirs.

❤It's nice to be important, but it's more important to be nice.

❤Everyone who has done the best he can is a hero.

❤No opportunity is ever lost. The other fellow takes those you miss.

❤It is easy enough to restrain our wrath when the other fellow is bigger.

❤You can always spot a well-informed man. His views are the same as yours.

❤It's not hard to spot a fool, unless he's hiding inside you.

❤The grass next door may look greener, but it's just as hard to cut.

❤Just think how happy you would be if you lost everything you now have, and then suddenly got it back.

❤The hope of the future lies in people who go to bed weary, instead of getting up all tired out.

❤The line between self-confidence and conceit is very narrow.

❤Gossip is one form of crime for which the law provides no punishment.

♥Gossip runs down as many persons as automobiles.

♥Talk is one thing of which the supply always exceeds the demand.

♥It is never wise to argue with a fool – the listeners don't know which is which.

♥One of the hardest secrets for a person to keep is his opinion of himself.

♥We've found you can always tell the host from the butler because the butler knows how to act.

♥The probable reason some people get lost in thought is because it is unfamiliar territory to them.

♥Nothing makes you more tolerant of a neighbor's party than being there.

♥The toughest form of mountain climbing is getting out of a rut.

♥It's no disgrace to be poor, and, besides, the installment salesmen leave you alone.

♥The person who rocks the boat is never the person at the oars.

♥To be a lady is a worthy trait, but it is a great handicap in an argument.

Parents & Kids

❤ Reluctantly bringing her precious child to kindergarten for his very first day of school, his mother explained to the teacher, "Kenny is so sensitive. Don't ever punish him. Just slap the boy next to him. That will frighten Kenny."

❤ During preliminary inspection at a Boy Scout camp, the director found an umbrella in the bedroll of a tiny Scout. Since the umbrella was obviously not one of the items of equipment listed, the director asked the boy to explain. The answer came, "Sir, did you ever have a mother?"

❤ *Mother:* (examining toy): "Isn't this rather complicated for a small child?"
Clerk: "It's an educational toy, Madam, designed to adjust a child to live in the world today. Any way he puts it together it's wrong."

❤ Sooner or later every woman must take a choice between motherhood and a career. Should she give the cereal boxtop to Jimmy to send for a compass, or should she keep it herself and enter the $10,000 contest?

❤ *Mother:* "Let's buy Junior a bicycle."
Father: "Do you think it will improve his behavior?"

Mother: "No, but it will spread his meanness over a wider area."

❤ A father, his arms filled with groceries, got on a bus with his son, about five.

The son had the fare and dropped it in the box, then seemed to feel he should explain. "I'm paying the money," he told the driver in a voice that carried clearly through the bus. "My father is loaded."

❤ The children were in a free-for-all when Dad entered the room. "Billie, who started this?" he asked the nearest boy.

"Well," replied Billie, "It all started when Frank hit me back."

❤ *Mother:* "Sit down, Tommy, and tell your sister a story."

Tommy: "Can't sit down, Mother, I just told Daddy a story."

❤ *Little boy* (in woodshed): "Father, you say grandpa spanked you and great-grandpa spanked grandpa, too?"

Father: "Yes."

Little boy: "Well, don't you think with my help you could overcome this inherited rowdyism?"

❤ The TV repairman was trying to find the trouble in a set. Just then the six-year-old came home from school. "I'll bet," he said, "if you'd clean out the dead cowboys from the bottom of the set, it would work again."

❤ The father played possum while his youngsters tried their best to rouse him from a Sunday afternoon nap to take them for a promised walk. Finally, his five-year-old daughter pried open one of his eyelids, peered carefully, then reported: "He's still in there."

❤ A child from the city slums was in the country for the first time. Everything he saw on the farm was new and wondrous to him.

Toward sunset of the first day he stood intently watching the farmer's wife plucking a chicken.

After a bit his curiosity grew too great and he asked gravely, "Do you take off their clothes every night, lady?"

❤ The Brown kids are rabid baseball fans, and everybody who knows the old man can understand why. Well, one day a kid in the neighborhood asked this question: "Suppose, Johnny, your father and the leading batter in the National League were both hanging from a cliff, about to drop off. Which one would you rescue first?"

"Are you kidding?" exclaimed little Johnny. "Why my father never hit .300 in his life!"

❤ While his birthday party was being planned, little Jimmie was asked for a list of friends he would like to invite to the party.

"I want Aunty Mills, Grandpa Smith, Uncle Dick and Grandma Jones, and…"

"But wait a minute, Jimmie. Everyone of those you have mentioned is an older person," said mother.

"Well," replied Jimmie, "they're the only ones who ever seem to have any money."

A boy was behaving badly. His mother said to him: "How do you ever expect to get into Heaven?" The boy replied: "Well, I'll just run in and out and keep slamming the door until St. Peter says, 'For heaven's sake, come in or stay out.'"

❤ Little Angus, given five dollars for his birthday, had the drugist change the bill into pennies, nickels and dimes. Then he went to another store and got a five dollar bill for the change, then to the third for change again. Asked by his father to explain, he replied: "Sooner or later somebody will make a mistake in the change – and it won't be me."

❤ A three-year old boy cried bitterly as a large friendly dog bounded up to him and licked his hands and face. "What is it?" asked his mother. "Did he bite you?"

"No," came the cry. "But he tasted me."

❤ A small boy went to a Sunday school picnic, but it hardly lived up to his expectations. He was stung by a bee; he fell into a creek; a little girl pulled his hair; he got badly sunburned. Late in the afternoon he reached home in an extremely disheveled state. As he limped up the front steps his mother greeted him and said:

"Well, son, what sort of a time did you have at the picnic?"

"Mama," slowly replied the little boy, "I'm so glad I'm back I'm glad I went."

❤ The boy scout remarked at the breakfast table, "I've already done my good deed for the day." His father replied, "You've been very quick about it."

"Yes, but it was easy," replied the boy. "I saw Mr. Smith going for the 7:45 train and he was afraid he'd miss it. So I let the bulldog loose, and he was just in time."

❤ A man was seated on a park bench when a little boy about five sat down beside him and started winding what appeared to be a most prized possession – a dollar watch.

"My what a pretty watch," the man remarked. "Does it tell you the time?"

"No, sir," replied the little fellow, "you gotta look at it."

❤ *Mother:* "Did you thank Mrs. Jones for the lovely party she gave?"

Mary: "No Mummy. The girl leaving just before me

thanked her, and Mrs. Jones said, 'Don't mention it,' so I didn't."

❤ *Son:* "Pop, what is creeping inflation?"
Father: "It's when your mother starts out asking for a new hat and winds up with a complete new outfit."

❤ A young boy of thirteen was waiting to get into the play, *Cats*, when he was spied by one of his father's friends.
"Hello, Paul," said the man. "How did you happen to get here tonight, you lucky kid!"
"Oh, I came on my brother's ticket," said the boy.
"And where's your brother?"
"Home looking for his ticket, I suppose," said Paul.

❤ All that keeps some people from having a home of their own is a popular teen-age daughter.

❤ *Farmer:* "Hi there! What are you doing up in my cherry tree?"
Youngster: "There's a sign down there says, 'Keep off the grass.'"

❤ *Mother* (trying to induce little daughter to go to bed early): "Why, even the little chickens go to bed at sundown."
Daughter: "Yes, but the old hen goes with them."

❤ "My Dad is an Eagle, a Moose, an Elk and a Lion," boasted one youngster.
"Yeah?" gasped his wide-eyed companion, "How much does it cost to see him?"

❤Not only the camel, but Johnnie also could do without water for eight days if his mother would let him.

82

❤Not only are the sins of the fathers visited upon the children, but now-a-days the sins of the children are visited upon the fathers.

❤My father had no problem with raising a large family. His secret? Every Sunday he insisted on an all-day family drive – while he stayed home and watched the ball game.

❤It's my own fault. All of my life I've worked and slaved to provide a safe and attractive home for our kids to grow up in, a friendly and hospitable place to bring their friends to, a secure and certain refuge against the storms and furies of the outside world. And now that they've grown up, they won't leave.

❤We had a fantastic vacation last year. We bought a new car, put all the kids in the back seat, and took a cruise.

❤I know a couple who took their four kids, three dogs and two cats and spent a month's vacation in their camper. They saved enough money to pay for the divorce.

❤Doctors say that rock music can be very damaging to vocal chords. Not of the singers. Of parents saying to their kids, "Turn that d_ _n thing down!"

❤How things change. My father caught me smoking and took me to the woodshed. I caught my son smoking and was glad it was tobacco.

❤I worry about my son. The kid's lost his last five jobs. I think he's in training to be a consultant.

❤When I was a kid, my mother always told me to wear clean underwear in case I got in an accident – and it's

I don't spend a lot of time worrying about what my kids
will be when they grow up. I'm too busy trying to figure
out what they are right now.

affected my entire life. To this day, I still have the feeling that if I'm in an accident the first three things the
cops are going to ask for are my driver's license, Blue
Cross card and shorts.

❤We have three grandchildren. Two are spoiled rotten
– and the third hasn't come to visit us yet.

❤When I was a Boy Scout, I always dreamed of helping
little old ladies across the street. Of course, in those
days when you were twelve years old, a little old lady
was Marilyn Monroe.

❤The custom of kissing children goodnight is dying
out; parents nowadays can't wait up for them.

Political

❤I already know how I am going to vote – very carefully

❤The lastest edition of *Who's Who In Politics* is printed in pencil.

❤I don't think the Mayor has a sense of humor. All I did was two jokes about him and the very next day our town had a new tow-away zone. My driveway.

❤The biggest problem with the world today is – everybody's fixing the blame and nobody's fixing the trouble.

❤Primaries are what separate the aspirants from the half-aspirants.

❤I didn't say the election was crooked. I just said it's the first time I ever saw an absentee ballot – from Amelia Earhart.

❤It's amazing how many politicians subscribe to the Braille System of Economics. They're always putting the touch on the taxpayers.

❤The best training for government is to be a member of your college rowing team. You're already used to looking one way and going another.

❤We have a very cautious Weather Bureau. For instance, on Monday they predicted a 70% chance of Tuesday.

❤They say no two snowflakes are alike. The White House has that same problem with policy statements.

❤Modern merchandising hasn't quite made it to Russia. You can tell that by the signs in department stores saying: IF YOU DON'T SEE WHAT YOU WANT – WANT WHAT YOU SEE!

❤If Noah lived today, he would never build an ark. He'd just put the Department of Energy in charge of rain.

❤You know why politicians aren't interested in solar energy? How do you tax the sun?

❤I don't know which we have to worry about more: Windfall profits on the part of the oil companies or windbag economics on the part of the Congress.

❤Roller-skating is the sport that allows you to stand absolutely still while hurtling towards disaster. It's a little like Congress.

❤Nature has four principal ways of thinning out the herd: Drought, famine, floods and primaries.

❤They say that the planet Saturn does a complete turn every ten hours. Big deal. So does the White House.

❤Our Congressman is really something. We sent him to Washington for six terms and he hasn't done a thing. No bills, no proposals, no investigations, no laws – I mean, he hasn't done *a thing*! That's why we keep sending him.

❤Surveys show the American people don't believe in the press, the government, big business – or surveys.

❤As President Clinton knows, there are two sides to every Issue – his and his.

I have this recurring nightmare: American scientists finally perfect solar power. Then the Arabs buy the sun.

❤In the Middle East they cut off the hands of thieves which would never do in the West. Can you imagine 5,000 politicians called Lefty?

❤Then there's the city employee who went for his annual physical and was told he needed a long, completely undisturbed rest. So he went back to work.

❤I wish we didn't have to vote for a President and a Vice President at the same time. I've never been lucky with exactas.

❤(FOR SPEAKERS AND TOASTMASTERS) Incidentally, there will be one minor change in the program tonight. A Congressman was going to begin the program but his office called to say he'd be delayed for five to ten – years.

❤Let us never lose sight of that ancient bit of wisdom: Them that can, do. Them that can't, teach. And them that can't do either, get a government grant.

❤Political conventions are where people who need no introduction are given ten minute ones by people who do.

❤I won't say anything about the candidates, but this might be the Election Day to close the polls and open the bars.

❤You have to admit that Billy Carter was really down to earth. The question is: How did he get down to earth and from what planet?

❤It isn't easy being Vice President of the United States. How can you tell if you're late for work?

❤I think this administration does have the know-how to solve the energy problem. Let's face it, any group that can make pennies out of dollars, can make oil out of shale.

❤In the Sixties, parents thought it would be great if their kids would grow up to be Senators and Congressmen. In the Seventies, they just hoped their kids would stay out of jail. But here it is 1987 and parents have learned how to compromise. Now they hope their kids will be either Senators or Congressmen *and* stay out of jail.

❤The 535 members of Congress are public servants – proving once again how hard it is to get decent help.

❤The big problem facing government today is how to

separate the truly needy from the newly greedy.

♥If God had really meant us to have Cabinet government, Moses would have come down from Mount Sinai with the Ten Secretaries.

♥A conservative is someone who wants to improve things just the way they were.

♥Remember the good old days when mail was delivered for three cents – instead of lost for 32¢?

♥I don't mind telling you, I was a little shocked when I heard what a Congressman did to his wife on the steps of the Capitol. I guess he ran out taxpayers.

♥April 15th is when taxpayers feel like a fire hydrant in the kennel of life.

♥I sure hope this new economic program is right. Sometimes I get the feeling that every time we start seeing the light at the end of the tunnel the government sends out for more tunnel.

♥Easter will be celebrated a little differently at the White House. Instead of inviting the press to watch eggs being rolled down the White House lawn – this year eggs are being invited to watch the press rolled down the White House lawn.

♥What can you really say about the new budget? It has something for everyone – debt, unemployment, bankruptcy.

♥Our speaker is a man who knows full well the price of success – ulcers, high blood pressure, hypertension, nervous tics. The people in his department have them all.

❤We're living in strange times. Did you see that Letter to the Editor in the morning's paper? It said: When it comes to the Middle East, it's time for all concerned people to stand up and be recognized! Signed – Anonymous.

❤Now I know what they mean by political unrest. When you see what they're doing in Washington, who can sleep?

❤Today we even have clubs for people with certain I. Q.s. The top two percent go into Mensa. The bottom two percent go into Congress.

❤He's smiled so much during this campaign, he has the only teeth in town with a tan.

❤He's one of those politicians who believes in talking straight from the shoulder. Unfortunately the brain is somewhat higher.

❤I loved that speech. Now I know what they mean by pulling the bull over your eyes.

❤Nowadays, if anybody said, "We have nothing to fear but fear itself!" – I'd fear for them.

❤This just in from Illinois: With six cemeteries still to be heard from – the election is still too close to call.

❤I read what our Congressman's fee for a speech is. What I'd like to know is what it would cost to get him to listen for an hour.

❤After the last election, I'm happy to report that at least one Congressman kept his promise. He ran on a jobs platform and after only one month in office – his wife got a job, his son got a job, his brother-in-law got a job, his uncle got a job.

❤The mob has never rubbed anyone out in City Hall and I just realized why. When in City Hall, has there ever been anyone who knows too much?

❤I am firmly convinced that if the good Lord had been aware of the income tax, Moses would have come down from Mount Sinai with the Ten Deductions.

❤Incidentally, there is no truth to the rumor that the White House is planning to put a brand new motto on the dollar bill: IN GOD WE TRUST. IT'S THE FEDERAL RESERVE WE'RE NOT TOO SURE ABOUT.

❤In a certain backward community, where shoes were mostly for Sunday wear, a candidate employed an un-usual electioneering technique. To each voter who turned a sympathetic ear to his campaign promises, he gave a single shoe, explaining, "You promise to vote for me, but I'm not so certain you will do it. So I'm giving you one shoe only. If I'm elected, I'll come back and give you the other one!" He was elected by a landslide.

❤Ernie Simon says: "Some political speeches are so bad they actually sound like the candidate had written them himself."

❤A politician will consider every way of reducing taxes except cutting expenses.

❤Fog, it is announced, can now be made to order. This will be no news to politicians.

❤This is another year when it won't be necessary to

fool all the people all the time – only in the fall election campaigns.

❤Few politicians die because of ideals, but a great many ideals die because of politicians.

❤If politicians were obliged to stand on the planks of their party platforms, they would be constructed better.

❤We wonder if those biologists who assert there isn't a perfect man on the globe ever heard a campaign speech?

❤If you want to know how much a man can't remember, call him as a witness to an automobile accident.

Public Speaking

❤Public speaking is a little like taking a vacation. It helps to know the right place to stop.

❤It's amazing how noisy an audience can be when you ask for quiet – and how quiet it can be when you ask for money.

❤I just figured out why the average prayer takes 30 seconds and the average conference three days. God listens.

❤Tonight we'll discuss one of the most pressing issues of our time: Where does weight go when you lose it?

❤This man has all the creativity of a Xerox machine.

❤I happen to know this man is independently wealthy. He just opened up a chain of garage sales.

❤I don't want to brag, but I know all the answers. My problem is matching them up to the right questions.

❤The Program Director really wasn't too sure how I'd do tonight. I asked him the capacity of this room. He said "It sleeps 300."

❤I want to thank you for those kind and complete remarks. As any speaker will tell you, the emcee they worry about most is the fellow who claims you need no introduction and then mispronounces your name.

❤I just hope I'm adequately prepared for this very im-

People keep asking me how I always manage to be in such good spirits. I owe it all to health food. Every morning I get up and drink the juice from three martinis.

portant occasion. Standing here tonight I feel a little like Moses with two tablets of stone and a ballpoint pen.

❤Our next guest is a man who really believes in the American Dream. You can tell he believes in the American Dream because every time he gives a speech he puts people to sleep!

❤What can we really say about our guest of honor tonight? He's the only man I know who signs his name with an X – and then misspells it.

❤Old? At his last birthday party, they lit the candles on

his cake, put a grill over it and cooked nine steaks and a rib roast.

❤Conceited? His nose is so high in the air, yesterday he inhaled a sparrow.

❤Rich? Who else do you know has Perrier on the knee?

❤Important? When he calls DIAL-A-PRAYER – he doesn't get a recording.

❤Swift? He'd need a cue card just to say, "Huh?"

❤Tonight we honor a man whose life is an open book – and you know the kind of book they're publishing these days.

❤It has been said that our guest of honor has the hands of a surgeon and that's true. They're always wrapped around a golf club.

❤AFTER A VERY LONG INTRODUCTION: Do you realize, if I were one of those speakers who needs no introduction, we would have been home by now?

❤I had a bad experience at a banquet last night. When the speaker said, "In conclusion," I left – and missed two-thirds of his speech.

❤A sinking feeling is what you get in the pit of your stomach when you reach into your pocket for the envelope that contains your speech and find the envelope that contains your 1040.

❤I won't say how many mistakes he's made during his 35 years with our company, but as a token of our esteem and admiration, we had his eraser bronzed.

❤This may sound immodest, but I have to agree with the Program Chairman that when it comes to speakers, I'm one of the best. Mostly because, to a Program Chairman, the best things in life are free.

❤(COMPANY ROAST): Tonight we honor a man who, throughout his thirty years with this company, was never too busy to see anyone. Mostly because he was never too busy.

❤In a loud and raucous world, he is a quiet man. He speaks softly, never lifts his hand in anger and is always ready to consider the other side in a dispute. If there were just one word to describe him, that word would be "chicken."

❤(DRUNK): Sir, you've reached Alcoholic. Would you now like to try for Anonymous?

❤(HECKLER): Sir, you have some wonderful thoughts but they haven't quite worked their way through to your mouth.

❤(FOR SPEAKERS AND TOASTMASTERS): It is a little intimidating to be here tonight. As I look around at this head table, I'm the only one up here I haven't heard of.

❤I once got a note on stationery that said FROM THE DESK OF THE CHAIRMAN OF THE BOARD. It was the first time I was ever fired by a desk.

❤Why is it that my body always feels older than I am?

❤RESPONDING TO A ROAST: First, I want to thank our previous speaker – sometimes known as the G. Gordon Liddy of comedy.

❤Astrologically speaking, I've never heard so much Taurus in all my life.

❤"In conclusion" – I love that phrase. It's like a wake-up call for audiences.

❤I'm sick and tired of waking up so sick and tired.

❤Send a dozen roses up to her, and pour four for me.

❤I only miss you on the days that end in "Y."

❤If today was a fish, I'd throw it back in.

❤How can whiskey six years old whip a person that's 32?

❤I may fall again, but I'll never get up this slow.

❤I'd rather have a bottle in front of me than a frontal lobotomy.

❤I had a terrible experience on my vacation. While I was downstairs telling the desk clerk I had lost my traveler's checks, somebody was upstairs stealing my cash.

❤Speeches are like pouring catsup from a bottle. You either get too little or too much.

❤After-dinner speeches go back to the very beginning of recorded time, when Adam said to Eve: "I don't think we shoulda done that."

❤Believe me, it's not easy to electrify a group that's already gassed.

❤You can always tell an audience that's spent a little too much time at the Happy Hour. When they try to clap – they miss.

❤He isn't cheap. He just has an impediment in his reach.

❤The problem in a lot of companies are workers who settle for early retirement – two years before they quit.

❤Whenever I hear a speaker say, "I hardly know where

to begin!" – something within me says, "Somewhere near the end."

❤There is one great mystery about hotels that may never be solved. How is it that when you want to sleep, they want to make up the room at 7 a.m.? And when you want to check in, they still haven't made up the room at 7 p.m.?

❤I've never had any luck with women. I can remember when I was six years old, I told the little girl next door I wanted to play doctor. She told me she was a Christian Scientist.

❤Looking back, there are so many memories. Who can ever forget that fateful day thirty years ago, when out of the 5,000 employees in our company, the Chairman of the Board took _____ aside – and left him there.

❤Retirement is when you finally find out what your spouse has been doing all day long – and you're sorry you asked.

❤INTERRUPTER: Sir, you have the right to remain silent. Why don't you use it?

❤I'm so unlucky, if I had been Abraham Lincoln and had written the Gettysburg Address on the back of an envelope – somebody would have mailed it.

❤Our son has reached that in-between stage of life. We can't quite decide if he's a late bloomer or an early retiree.

❤The Republicans have finally come up with the answer to the question: "What do you give to the person who everything?" More.

❤Delivering a speech is like spelling Mississippi. You're never quite sure when to stop.

❤I'm firmly convinced that what the airport needs is one more commuter airline. Something that'll get us from the terminal to the gate.

❤Do you realize we've had the 55 mile per hour speed limit for years now – and the only one who's still observing it is the airline?

❤Personally, I don't relate to the traditional view of Hell as being fire and brimstone. To me, Hell would be, for all eternity, flying (*any name*) Airline – economy class – in a middle seat - during a typhoon – immediately after they've served the coffee.

❤The best retirement is when you have the whole day to do nothing in – and it isn't enough.

❤AFTER A FAUX PAS: I'm sorry. Sometimes I say what I'm thinking before I think what I'm saying.

❤CLOSING: And so, let me just leave you with these words of wisdom I once heard at Women's Lib: "When Mrs. Hutton talks, E.F. listens!"

❤Being fashionable is always a problem. How do you put last year's hips into this year's clothes?

❤You know you're getting older when you light the candles on your birthday cake – and the air-conditioning switches on.

❤You know your team's in trouble when the pitching machine throws a no-hitter.

❤ABOUT A GUEST WHO ALWAYS DRESSES CA-

SUALLY: You can tell he's taken this occasion rather seriously. His socks match.

❤Our next guest is a man so unknown, even his American Express card doesn't help.

❤IF YOU GARBLE A SENTENCE: That's called a Neutron Sentence. It destroys the meaning but leaves the words intact.

❤An awards banquet is where they say grace and then the losers eat their hearts out.

❤I don't want to brag, but I really have only one worry – that St. Peter is going to say I'm overqualified.

❤Our guest tonight is a true conservative. For those of you who aren't sure what a true conservative is – it's anyone who has jockey shorts with cuffs.

❤People are very sneaky in this town. I was sitting in the lobby when this georgeous female sat down beside me and whispered, "Are you looking for some company?" I said, "Yes." And she sold me 300 shares of an over-the-counter stock.

❤Before we go any further, I'd also like my spouse to stand up and take a bow. (LEAD APPLAUSE AND THEN LOOK AROUND AS NO ONE STANDS UP, SHAKE YOUR HEAD AND COMMENT:) You know, after that last gas station, I thought the car was kinda quiet.

❤QUIETING AN AUDIENCE: Could we have a little quiet in the back, please? There are people up here trying to sleep.

❤Our next guest has been called a self-made man. This,

of course, was in the days before quality control.

❤I'm so busy, if I had my life to live over again, I'd need more time.

❤Things haven't been easy for our next guest. As you all know, last year his company had to relocate – and he's still trying to find out where.

❤I'm easily intimidated. Yesterday my dog hit me with a rolled-up newspaper.

❤In introducing our Treasurer, the good news is – he's honest as the day is long. The bad news is – for the last five years he's been working the night shift.

❤St. Patrick's Day is when some people celebrate by downing a bottle of Irish whiskey. Some celebrate by downing three bottles of Irish whiskey. And then, there are those who overdo it.

❤What can you really say about ___, I worship the water he walks on.

❤RESPONDING TO SOMEONE WHO HAS JUST ROASTED YOU: First, I want to thank the previous speaker – a man of many talents. As you can see, humor isn't one of them.

❤One baseball player is being paid so much money, when he hits a homer he doesn't run the bases — he sends for them.

❤WHEN YOU GET AN AWARD: I'm kinda embarrassed getting this honor because I really am a very modest person. An extremely modest person. A tremendously talented and wonderfully deserving modest person.

101

❤Every employee who golfs knows how important the fundamentals are. Like keeping your head down – when the boss throws his ball out of the rough.

❤A sensitive, compassionate, caring man – he is best known as the creator of our company's motto: IF AT FIRST YOU DON'T SUCCEED – OUT!

❤The boss never loses his temper. He can always find it when he needs it.

❤INTRODUCTION: Through the years our company has experienced a lot of growing pains – and tonight we have one of them with us.

❤In all fairness to the previous speaker, he is recovering from major surgery. Had a talent bypass.

❤What can I tell you? That was a speech to be remembered. Not repeated. Just remembered.

❤Have you been to the bar yet? They serve very interesting drinks – 10% alcohol, 40% ice and 50% tip.

❤This man is so likeable – dogs come up and pet him.

❤Eat? They don't call him the fastest gums in the West for nothing.

❤I'll tell you what kind of an eater this man is. When he drives home from work and pulls into his driveway, he presses a little button on the dashboard of his car – and his refrigerator automatically opens.

❤A roast is when all is said and fun.

❤A very humble man. A very unobtrusive man. A very democratic man. He doesn't want anyone calling him sir. Kneeling is enough.

❤You overhear such interesting conversation at conven-

Two Roman galleys are lined up side by side for the start of the Emperor's annual race down the Tiber, One galley slave turns to another and says, "Let's win this one for the Whipper!"

tions – like: "I'm getting a little worried about Harry. Yesterday he went into the hotel restaurant and asked for the wine list."

"Lots of people go into the hotel restaurant and ask for the wine list."

"For breakfast?"

♥During the war, he served his country in the Pentagon. What he served his country was breakfast, lunch and dinner.

♥When it comes to being an unqualified success you just can't beat the boss's son.

❤And now, it gives me great pleasure to bring this session to a close. One more hour and I would have asked _____ to free us.

❤I really shouldn't kid about the boss because he just had a heart operation. They put one in.

❤Wasn't that great? What a remarkable speech for a man who still thinks Taco Bell is the Mexican phone company.

❤CLOSING: I have a lot more to say but I always try to observe the first rule of public speaking: Nice guys finish fast!

Put Downs

❤*Mrs. A to Mrs. B.*: "It's a beautiful picture of her, except that the retouch man has made a liar out of the camera."

❤To be a balanced citizen you must spend some time each day trying to keep up with the national and international news, even though you are more interested in some local scandal.

❤It was lunch hour at the plant, and Pat's two buddies decided to play a joke on him during his absence. They drew the features of a donkey on the back of his coat. Pat returned and presently came into sight bearing the decorated coat.

"What's the trouble, Pat?" asked one casually.

"Not much," replied Pat. "I'd like to know just which one of yez wiped your face on me coat!"

❤*First boarder*: "This cheese is so strong it could walk over and say 'Hello' to the coffee."

Second boarder: "Yes, but the coffee is too weak to answer back."

❤A lady was entertaining her friend's small son.

"Are you sure you can cut your meat?" she asked, after watching his struggles.

"Oh, yes," he replied. "We often have it as tough as

this at home."

❤Mrs. Jones swept into the meeting of the Ladies' Aid society. She was in a huff and she stormed across to Mrs. Smith.

"Did you tell Mrs. Brown I was nothing but a gossip?" demanded Mrs. Jones.

Mrs. Smith's eyebrows raised in mild surprise. "Why, no," she answered. "I thought Mrs. Brown knew."

❤During a pause in a long, tiring speech, one guest said to another: "What follows this speaker?"

Second guest: "Wednesday."

❤The town was so backward that they even voted for Calvin Coolidge. I know lots of people did – but last year.

❤"Sir, my stenographer, being a lady, cannot type what I think of you. I, being a gentleman, cannot think it. You, being neither, will understand just what I mean."

❤The horn-tooter in traffic was squelched by a lady pulling up alongside his car and inquiring, very sweetly, "What else did you get for Christmas?"

❤A doctor asked the woman patient her age.

"I never tell anyone my age," she answered, "but as a matter of fact, I've just reached twenty-five."

"Indeed," said the doctor, "what detained you?"

❤A clever young lady was asked to attend a public function. She was given a place between a noted bishop and an equally famous rabbi. It was her chance to break into high company, and she meant to make use of it.

"I feel as if I were a leaf between the Old and the New

Testament," she said during a lull in the conversation. "That page, Madam," said the rabbi, "is usually a blank."

❤Heard in the radio studios: He's smarter than he looks – but then he'd have to be."

❤*Mrs. No. 1*: "That's a very lovely coat your're wearing, Mrs. Jones.

Mrs. No. 2: "Oh, thank you. My husband gave it to me for my thirty-fifth birthday."

Mrs. No. 1: "It certainly wears well, doesn't it!"

❤Ugly? She has the only mirror in town that winces!

❤Amateur shows are a means for people with no talent to prove it.

❤An after-dinner speaker rose to speak. "After partaking of such a meal," he continued, "I feel, if I had eaten another bite, I would be unable to speak." From the far end of the table came an order to the waiter: "Give him a sandwich."

❤Sir, has it ever occurred to you that you might be ten minutes ahead in your talking and an hour behind in your listening?

❤In all these years, I have never heard anyone say one bad word about him. It usually took several paragraphs.

Religion

♥A little old lady handed the post office clerk a package containing a Bible.

"Anything breakable in this?" he asked.

"Nothing but the Ten Commandments," the little lady replied.

♥Over in South London town in Canada during the holiday season an enthusiastic Salvation Army girl-lieutenant was going from door to door with the collection box. She went to the door of a good old lady and asked if she would like to help the carolers.

"I'd love to dearie," replied the old lady, rather creakily, "but I've got the bronchitis something terrible this year, and I couldn't sing a note."

♥Bishop Fulton J. Sheen was on the air receiving a special award for the excellence of his program. In acknowledging it, he stated that he thought writers often deserved credit for TV programs but rarely got it. So he gave credit to – Matthew, Mark, Luke, and John.

♥A Scotchman had been told by his doctor that he had a floating kidney. Disturbed by the diagnosis, he went to the pastor of his church with a request for the prayers of the congregation.

"I'm afraid," the pastor said, "that the mention of a

floating kidney would cause the congregation to laugh."

"Only last Sunday you prayed for loose livers," said the Scotchman.

❤One place people seem to think they can get just as much as ever for a dollar is in church.

❤The fellow who argues that all religions should unite probably doesn't speak to his brother-in-law.

❤No one can ever doubt the miracles who sees a minister living on a salary fixed ten years ago, and keeping out of debt.

❤It's a little difficult to reconcile the creed of some Christians with their greed.

❤"Oh, Mother!" cried Jimmie excitedly. "There's a big black bear in the backyard!"

"You know perfectly well it's only a big dog," said his mother.

"Now go to your room and ask God to forgive you for telling a lie."

"Did you ask God to forgive you?" she said, when Jimmie came downstairs a little later.

"Yes," he replied, "and He said it was all right. He thought it was a bear Himself the first time He saw it."

❤"Folks," said the old minister, "the subject this evening is 'Liars.' How many in the congregation have read the 69th chapter of Matthew?"

Nearly every hand in the audience was raised.

"That's right," said His Reverence. "You are the ones

I want to preach to. There is no 69th chapter of Matthew!"

❤Two ministers of different faiths were the best of friends, but they often disagreed on religious questions. One day they had been arguing, a little more than usual, on some theological point, when one of them said, "That's all right. We'll just agree to disagree. The thing that counts is that we're both doing the Lord's work, you in your way and I in His."

❤Someone the other day was telling me about a youngster who asked his mother this question: "If the Lord gives us our daily bread and Santa Claus brings the Christmas presents and the stork brings the babies, then what's the use of having Daddy around?"

❤Some persons think if they wear their best clothes on Sunday they're observing the Sabbath.

❤Some persons never appeal to God unless they're getting licked.

❤A real atheist is someone who doesn't even believe in bingo.

❤Our church has a rather unusual problem. The minister just asked for Sundays off.

❤I'm not saying this man is a bad reporter. All I'm saying is, if he had been Moses, what we'd have today is The Six Commandments.

❤And so it came to pass that the United Kingdom elected its first woman prime minister – and the Lord looked down and said, "Good! That makes two of us!"

❤I never really believed God is a woman until I called DIAL-A-PRAYER and kept getting a busy signal.

❤I'm just glad Moses didn't come down from Mount Sinai today. I mean, how would that sound? "Thank you for not killing." "Thank you for not stealing." "Thank you for not coveting your neighbor's wife."

❤It must be wonderful to be the Pope. To be able to call up DIAL-A-PRAYER and ask, "Any messages?"

❤It's very hard to be an unbeliever. For instance, Jesus said the poor will always be with us – and that was 2,000 years before Chrysler.

❤You never know enough nuns.

❤I've just joined that new religious group that doesn't believe in getting involved. Maybe you've heard of it – Jehovah's Bystanders.

❤In a world of doubt, uncertainty and questioning, he is a religious man. Says grace before every martini.

❤God created the world in six days and on the seventh day, He rested. Then, on the eighth day, He started to answer the complaints.

School Days

❤The newly engaged kindergarten teacher was justly proud of her of her sparkling diamond and enjoyed showing the stone to all who asked to see it. Bruce, one of her pupils, asked to see it one day, and then inquired, "Is it a real ring?"

"Why, certainly," replied the teacher.

"Well, then," he said, "let's see it squirt water."

❤"What," asked the teacher, "was the title for the former rulers of Russia?"

"Czar," replied a student.

"And the title for his wife?" the teacher continued.

"The Czarina."

"That's right," said the teacher, "and for his children?" The student thought a minute and replied, "Czardines?"

❤"If your mother gave you a large apple and a small apple and told you to share with your brother, which one would you give him?" asked the teacher.

"Do you mean my little brother or my big brother?" asked the pupil.

❤*Teacher*: "Johnny, can you tell me what a grudge is?"
Johnny: "A grudge is a place where they keep automobiles."

❤The teacher played the *Star Spangled Banner* and asked her class to identify it. "That's easy," shouted a pupil. "It's what they play just before the ballgame."

❤*Teacher*: "Johnny, how do you spell 'imbecile'?"
Johnny: "I-m-b-u-s-s-u-l."
Teacher: "The dictionary spells it 'i-m-b-e-c-i-l-e.'"
Johnny: "Yeah. But you asked me how I spelled it."

❤Safety slogan: "Watch out for school children – especially if they are driving cars."

❤The most common impediment of speech today in children is often bubble gum.

❤The teacher had asked the class to list, in their opinion, the eleven greatest Americans. After a while she stopped at one desk and asked:
"Have you finished your list yet, Bobby?"
"Not yet, teacher," Bobby replied. "I can't decide on the fullback."

❤Sally, a kindergarten pupil, was learning the alphabet. "What comes after T?" asked the teacher.
The little girl didn't hesitate a minute. "V," she replied.

❤The teacher asked his pupils to write an essay telling what they would do if they had a million dollars.
Every pupil except little Willie began writing immediately. Willie sat idle, twiddling his fingers and watching the flies on the ceiling.
The teacher collected the papers, and Willie handed in a blank sheet.
"How is this, Willie?" asked the teacher. "Is this your

You want to know what our kids are like? I'll tell you what our kids are like. Our sixteen-year-old we call Attila the Son.

essay? All the other pupils have written two sheets or more while you have done nothing!"

"Well," replied Willie, "that's what I'd do if I had a million dollars!"

♥A chrysanthemum by any other name would be easier to spell.

♥A first grade teacher knows how to make little things count.

♥*Teacher* (patiently): "If one and one makes two, and two and two makes four, how much does four and four make?

Pupil: "That ain't fair, teacher. You answer the easy

ones yourself and leave the hard ones for me."

❤*Teacher*: "Willie, what happened in the year 1732?"
Willie: "George Washington was born."
Teacher: "And what happened in 1776?"
Willie: "George Washington was forty-four years old."

❤It was Junior's first day in school, and when he got home his mother asked, "Did you learn anything today?"

"No," he replied in disgust. "I have to go back tomorrow."

❤When you criticize your child for not being smart, remember a wooden head is one thing that can be inherited.

❤*Tom*: "Say, Bill, how did you get that swelling on your nose?"
Bill: "Oh, I bent down to smell a brose in my garden."
Tom: "Not brose, Bill, rose. There's no 'B' in rose."
Bill: "There was in this one."

❤If they ever do away with comic books, many American youngsters will quit reading.

❤Can you spell expediency in five letters? Yes, XPDNC.

❤A schoolboy was making a speech on the national debt. He said: "It's too bad that future generations can't be here at this time to see the wonderful things we're doing with their money."

❤Asked to define "memory," one youngster replied sagely, "The thing I forget with."

❤*Teacher*: "Yes, Johnny, what is it?"

Johnny: "I don't want to scare you, but Papa said if I don't get better grades someone is due for a licking."

❤"I'm warning you," said the exasperated piano teacher to the young boy. "If you don't behave yourself, I'll tell your parents you have talent!"

❤A safety sign read: "School – Don't Kill a Child." Beneath this admonition was written in a childish scrawl: "Wait for a Teacher."

❤"How does it happen that you are five minutes late for school this morning?" the teacher asked severely. "Please, ma'am, I must have overwashed myself."

❤Little Rosalie, a first-grader, walking with her mother, spoke to a small boy. "His name is Jimmy, and he is in my class," she explained.
"What is the little boy's last name?" her mother asked.
"His whole name," said Rosalie, "is Jimmy Sitdown – that's what the teacher calls him."

❤*First student*: "Ya like to read, don't-cha?"
Second student: "Sure!"
First student: "Whatcha like to read?"
Second student: "Oh, Superman, Garfield and Mickey Mouse."

❤As the little boy says, "Ignorance is when you don't know something, and somebody finds it out."

❤It's amazing. Yesterday our twelve year old came home from camp with a six week accumulation of dirty laundry. What makes it so amazing – it was a three week camp.

❤I'm really getting concerned about our educational

system. At one high school, the senior voted MOST LIKELY TO SUCCEED didn't graduate.

❤Yesterday I told my son to do his homework, pay attention in class, study real hard and someday he might be President of the United States. He said, "Don't threaten me!"

❤June is the best month to determine a kid's future. It all depends on whether he's leaving school to begin a vacation – or to continue one.

❤One of my kids has been looking for a job religiously. Every morning he turns to the Want Ads for three minutes, says Amen and goes to the beach.

❤"In space no one can hear you scream." What a great place to raise kids.

❤It is the studying that you do after your school days that really counts. Otherwise, you know only that which everyone else knows.

❤My kid got very upset at his commencement ceremony. The speaker said, "The world is yours!" – and he hates to be threatened.

❤June is when a graduate goes out to set the world on fire. July is when he starts to wonder if maybe his matches are wet.

❤May is when a kid goes to a commencement exercise and is told the future is his. June is when he goes to an employment agency and is told the present is not.

❤City kids have difficult time understanding the Christmas story. When I said that Mary and Joseph had to spend the night in a stable, my daughter asked, "What's a stable?" I said, "Picture your room without the stereo!"

❤Raising kids is a peculiar business. You spend half your time trying to instill them with knowledge – and the other half telling them not to be so damn smart!

❤I admit it. I'm in my second childhood. Now I'm working my son's way through college.

❤The hardest job a modern writer has is communicating with kids. How do you get a T-shirt into a typewriter?

❤There's only one way to keep kids from seeing dirty movies: Label them EDUCATIONAL.

❤There is no substitute for higher education. For instance, my son can now explain in six different languages why he can't find a job.

❤You can lead a boy to college, but you cannot make him think.

❤Nowadays kids just have to go to college. How else are they going to get a good high school education?

❤*Coach to football lineman*: "You're out of condition again, Jones. What'cha been doing, studyin'?"

❤*Freshman*: "How about a battle of wits?"
Senior: "Sorry, I never attack an unarmed man."

❤*Professor*: "What is the principal contribution of the automobile age?"
Freshman: "Well, it's practically stopped horse stealing."

❤*University dean*: "Why do you want to be a pharmacist?"

Student: "Well, my dad is one. He works seven days a week and it's our family ambition to give him a day off."

❤You can lead high school graduates to college, but you cannot make them think.

❤College professors are the persons who get what's left after the athletic director and football coach are paid off.

❤The aim of education is to enable a man to continue his learning.

❤A prof was retiring after teaching mathematics for fifty years. He was building a lodge in the mountains in which to spend his declining years.

"Have you named it yet?" his friend asked.

"Oh, yes," said the prof. "I'm calling it 'After Math.'"

❤On his way out of the lecture the professor asked if anyone had seen his hat.

"You're wearing it, sir," a student replied.

"Thank you," said the professor. "If you hadn't seen it, I'd have gone home without it."

Sports

❤*Golfer* (in trap): "The traps on this course are quite annoying, aren't they?"

Second golfer (trying to putt): "They sure are. Would you mind closing yours?"

❤*Golfer*: "You must be the worst caddy in the world!"

Caddy: "Oh, no sir. That would be too much of a coincidence."

❤The golfer teed up, eyed the distance to the green and announced: "A drive and a putt will do it."

Then he swung – but the ball traveled only a few yards. His caddie handed him the putter, remarking brightly: "This putt will be worth telling the boys about."

❤Went to the baseball game with my wife. One fellow hit the ball over the fence, and she said, "I'm glad they got rid of it; now we can go home."

❤Before you call yourself peace-loving, tell us how you act when the umpire calls a close one on the home team.

❤*Golfer* (in a thicket): "Never mind about my ball, caddie. Come and find me!"

❤*Fan*: "How about your team? Are they good losers?"

Coach: "Good? Heck, they're perfect."

❤Fisherman's Motto – Bait and See.

❤For some persons it is simply life, liberty and the pursuit of a golf ball.

❤The big game hunter was missing in Africa. Apparently something he disagreed with ate him.

❤College football makes hardy young people. You can't sit three hours on cold concrete, eating a cold hot dog and peanuts and be a weakling.

❤The professors who complain that football interferes with academic work don't realize how seriously academic work interferes with football.

❤Our new golf pro watched my game and then gave me the best advice ever for improving my golf score. He said all I have to do is four things: Keep my head down, my eyes on the ball, my left arm straight, and cheat.

❤To cut ten strokes off your golf score, all you have to do is get rid of one thing – witnesses.

❤Hockey is a very strange game. A very physical game. A very violent game. I mean, I know a professional hockey player who got mugged three times last month – and still doesn't know it.

❤Fishing is probably the most fun a person can have without having much fun.

❤And it's a very competitive college. Even the debating team takes steroids.

When some persons trade in their cars, they should go to the abused car lot.

Transportation

❤Don't get discouraged and sell your car. Any day now you may find a place to park it.

❤Traffic is so bad that even back seat drivers can't help much.

❤A great many drivers seem to think the speed limit on a highway is what their cars can do.

❤In most cities traffic is so jammed motorists sit in their cars and watch the pedestrians whiz by.

❤The driver is safer when the roads are dry, the roads

are safer when the driver is dry.

❤The hand that lifts the cup that "cheers," should not be used to shift the gears.

❤Said the man of tall tales, "My wife is the safest driver in the world – she drives in the safety zone."

❤A careful driver is something more than a guy who honks his horn as he goes through a red light.

❤Once upon a time, and not more than that, a son asked for the garage keys, and came out with the lawn mower.

❤*Mechanic*: "Which do you prefer, leather or fabric auto upholstering?"

Second Mechanic: "I like fabric; leather is too hard to wipe your hands on."

❤When a major highway is open, it's probably because they're repairing the detour.

❤Many a husband argues with his wife about which fork to use when a highway divides.

❤Sign on a highway in Connecticut: "Crossroad ahead, better humor it."

❤Judging from the way some fellows drive, if the road turns the same time they do, it's a coincidence.

❤Isn't it terrible how close some motorists drive ahead of you?

❤Sign on a country road: "Drive carefully; there isn't a hospital within 50 miles."

❤It's easy to die with your boots on, if they're on the accelerator.

❤There are two kinds of finishes you can put on an automobile – lacquer and liquor.

❤I had a problem last week so I went up to see the Supervisor Of Baggage. I knew it was the Supervisor Of Baggage because he had a whole roomful of people calling him by the initials.

❤I like flying. It's always a fascinating experience to sit in a big airport and watch the planes take off – and wonder which one of them has your luggage.

❤Remember your first flight and how you spent the entire time looking out the window – watching, listening and worrying about the engine? Remember your last flight and how you spent the entire time looking out the window – watching, listening and worrying about the engine?

❤A Brooklyn gentleman took his wife to the Newark Airport and put her on a plane for Buffalo. After fighting his way through the traffic, he arrived back home and wearily ascended the steps to his home, to find a telegram in his mailbox. He opened it and read, "Arrived safely love Lulu."

Women

❤The modern woman doesn't want a man who can satisfy her smallest wish; what she wants is one who can attend to the larger ones.

❤Women are not strong physically, but one of them can put the cap on a fruit jar so it takes 20 minutes for her husband to get it off.

❤The proper study of mankind is not man but woman.

❤"What do the ruins of Ancient Egypt really prove?" wonders a writer. Probably, among other things, that Ancient Egyptian wives insisted on having a shot at backing the chariot into the garage.

❤Most women are as pretty this year as they were five years ago, but it takes quite a little longer.

❤Women will never be men's equal until they can sport a bald spot, on top of their heads, and still think they're handsome.

❤Progress – In the old days a girl got her good looks from her mother. Now she gets it from the beauty parlor.

❤No woman ever makes a fool out of a man without his full cooperation.

❤The average girl would rather have beauty than brains, because she knows that the average man can see better than he can think.

❤A woman keeps a secret she doesn't know.

❤A woman, provided she knows that her hat is on straight, is prepared to look the whole world in the face at any moment.

❤Many a young man who asks for a girl's hand later finds himself under her thumb.

❤If a wife doesn't treat her husband as she should, he should be thankful.

❤"After the Bawl Was Over," she got her new fur coat.

❤Why should he worry about who's boss at home. He'll be happier if he never finds out.

❤A gentleman is a man who holds the door open for the wife while she carries in a load of groceries.

❤Generally the bride looks stunning and the groom stunned.

❤If you notice a urinal in the ladies' room, you have probably made a mistake.

❤Women can work as fast as men. They just have to slow down.